New Perspectives on Psychology and Religion

Rev. Dr. Tom Bush

PublishAmerica
Baltimore

First printing

At the specific preference of the author, PublishAmerica allowed this work to remain exactly as the author intended, verbatim, without editorial input.

ISBN: 1-4241-0148-4
PUBLISHED BY PUBLISHAMERICA, LLLP
www.publishamerica.com
Baltimore

Printed in the United States of America

To [illegible] Best Wishes [illegible] August 2006

Dedication

This book is dedicated to the congregations of Boscobel and Steuben Churches in Wisconsin, USA, who gave me the opportunity and time to write this book whilst I ministered to them for a year in 2004. They took a stranger into their midst and made me feel one of them. For the time and opportunity that they gave, I shall be eternally thankful.

I also dedicate this book to my wife, who allowed me to go to the USA whilst she stayed at home. For her love and support, I also give thanks.

Index

Chapter 1:

THE STUDY OF PSYCHOLOGY

What is psychology?

Of all the sciences Psychology is the one that most people think they know a lot about whilst, in fact, knowing very little. The reason for this is that psychology looks at what we see in people every day; their behavior, attitudes and perceptions. The difference between how a member of the general public and how a psychologist looks at people is that the psychologist does this in a systematic scientific way. Thus, if we are to give a definition to Psychology we can say that it is the scientific study of behavior and experience. Psychology is devoted to collecting facts about behaviour and experience and systematically organizing such facts into psychological theories. These theories aid in understanding and explaining people's behaviour and sometimes in predicting and influencing their future actions.

The study of psychology is often confused with ***psychiatry.*** This is mainly due to the fact that in popular fiction and television series a psychologist is called into to explain the abnormal behaviour of a person, behaviour that is often confused with mental disorder. So we need to make it clear at the outset that whilst psychology looks at behaviour, psychiatry studies the abnormal mind. The abnormal mind produces mental disorders that affect the behaviour and perceptions of the individual and, in the main, can be treated. Thus psychiatry is a branch of medicine. Psychiatrists diagnose and treat, often with drugs and physical therapies. Psychologists, who are not medical doctors, concentrate on observation and experimentation to understand our behaviour and how experience affects it. Only in the field of clinical psychology, where the psychologist works closely with medical profession, does one see psychologists involved in therapy. Often this is through group and individual consultations and does not involve the administration of drugs or physical intervention, for which they are not qualified.

Thus, as part of the human condition, understanding psychology can help in explaining the religious experience. One's religious belief, or absence of it, can and does have an effect one's attitude and behaviour. Most people who claim to be religious try to live their lives by a particular code of conduct. Whilst keeping to that code can lead to a contented and fulfilled life breaking it could lead to frustration and feelings of inadequacy all of which have an effect on behaviour and our attitude to other people and the world in general.

The Scope of Psychological Study

By accepting that psychology is the study of behaviour and experience on in humans one can imagine that the scope of study is quite vast. It ranges from understanding human development, speech and language, through how we perceive the world and learn from it, to how we remember and think. The concentration of study is always on explaining who we are and how we became who we are and how that inner understanding affects our behaviour in our daily lives.

A good way to look at the subject areas covered by the study of psychology is to find an introductory book on the subject and look at the chapter headings. By looking at the list of chapter headings one can get a feel for the subject areas that psychology covers

Reader's Activity:

At this point you might like to go to a library and find some books entitled "an introduction to psychology" and make a list of the chapter headings. Note the similarities in these headings. You might also like to note the differences.

In the main one will find that these subject heading can be split into four main groups, the biological, behaviour, social and abnormal. In so doing the authors of these introductions are taking the vast subject area covered by psychology and attempting to categorize the study into these key subject area. So let's take a closer look at these areas.

The Biological

This area of psychological study looks at the brain and how the neurobiological processes that take place in the brain affect our behaviour and mental processes. Much of this work has been greatly helped by the ability to conduct M.R.I. imaging of the brain whilst undertaking psychological tasks. From this researchers are able to learn which brain structures underlie the phenomena being studies. A good example of this is the work undertaken by Andrew Newberg who has been using imaging of the brain in relation to prayer and meditation. His work, which will be looked at in more detail in a later chapter, has demonstrated that the acts of prayer and meditation do have an effect on the brain activity. The biological study of the brain and behaviour has also allowed a much great understanding in looking at memory and perception as well as language development.

The Behavioral

A review of chapters under this heading will have revealed that the behavioral perspective of the study of psychology focuses heavily on observation and studying how behaviour is affected by conditioning and reinforcement. For example, your behaviour in relation to holding a burning match and watching the flame come nearer the fingers has been conditioned by previous experience. At some point in your life you will have been burnt by a match. The act of burning your fingers is a referred to a **negative** reinforcement. Thus, when this looks likely to happen again you will blow out the match to save yourself from being burnt. You have learnt how to behave in that given situation. Such observational studies have also been used to look at why people do or do not attend worship. Where it is positively reinforced, i.e. it is felt to be rewarding and meaningful, the person will continue to attend, whilst if it is felt to be negatively reinforced, i.e. old fashioned and boring, the person is put off attending again.

The Social

In our opening definition you will have noticed the word "Experience". In looking at behaviour it is almost impossible to overstate the effect that the environment has on the individual. Social psychologists mainly study how the social world that we live in affects our emotions, behaviour and, important for this book, our beliefs about the world and the influence that others have on shaping those beliefs. Often these influences affect a key component of what we think of as "ourselves" namely our personality. So, by looking at the family, the social setting and culture that we are brought up in, we can explain how our knowledge of ourselves and the world we live in is shaped. In the main such studies are done by observation but there have been some attempts in the past to use controlled environmental experiments to see how behaviour is changed. We will look at some of these experiments in later chapters

The Abnormal

As said earlier, it is at this point that psychology comes near to psychiatry. Abnormal psychology looks at what is called "maladaptive" behaviour. This is behaviour that has adverse effects on the individual or society in which that individual lives. For example people who have abnormal fears can get to a stage where those fears affect the quality of their lives. Whilst a psychiatrist would possible treat the fear with drugs or physical therapy, the psychologist would use behaviour based training programes to change the behaviour. Often maladaptive behaviour affects our perception or reality, our ability to control our behaviour acceptably, our self esteem as well as our relationships with others. It is possible to find people who display an excessive zeal in their religious observance that will adversely affect their relationships and daily living. In all other aspects they could be considered "normal"; holding down a job and ordering their lives in a socially acceptable way. This should not be confused with a person thinking they are god or another character from their religion. This is a psychiatric disorder relating the psychotic mind.

Schools of Psychology

From the above a number of key areas of study have developed which have affected the ways in which various subjects are looked at. Any topic in psychology can be studied from different perspectives. Often these studies compliment each other but in some cases these perspectives clash. A good example of this the development of behaviour. Do we learn how to behave by nature or nurture? In other words is behaviour passed on to us by genetic inheritance of through what we learn at our mother's knee? Depending on your perspective will determine how you answer such a question. So let's take a closer look at some of these perspectives.

The Psychobiological

As hinted at earlier, the psychobiological perspective believes that all behaviour has a neural basis. As the brain controls all body activity it must also control all our behavioural activity. The biological approach attempts to match behaviour to electrical and chemical activity in the brain. Put at its simplest all physical and mental activity must have a centre in the brain that initiates, controls and stops it. The aim of research is, thus to find where these centre are. For example, where does memory lie? Is it at a particular centre or is it stored within the area where such activity takes place, For example, our memory for a particular face could be linked with the optic centre in the brain. One of the ways to study this would be to observe people with damage to the optic centre in the brain and see how this affects memory of faces.

As stated earlier one of the most valuable tools in such research has been the development of the ability to scan the brain whilst carry out psychological tasks, commonly referred to as M.R.I. or magnetic resonance imaging. This has produced fantastic color images of the brain at work and, in so doing, is providing the key to understanding a whole range of psychological activity.

The Cognitive

The work cognition meant the ability to link things together like cogs in a mechanism which describes this perspective of psychology rather well. In the main it is concerned with the mental mechanisms that underpin thinking reasoning and the ability to problem solve. Psychologists break down such activity into stages. For example, in looking at memory it is possible to define various stages in the process namely, encoding, storage, retrieval. Encoding describes the process of putting the memory into the brain through our senses, storage looks at how the brain holds such information and retrieval looks at how and what stimulates us to remember.

The Behaviorists

This perspective believes that most behaviour can be explained through the idea of stimulus and response. This idea is one of the oldest in the study of behaviour and has within its ranks such famous psychology as Pavlov, (a name that often rings a bell) and B.F. Skinner both of who with the use or positive and negative reinforcement changed animals and, later, human behaviour.

A strict behavioural approach does not, as in cognitive psychology, consider the individual mental processes, but rather the way that the individual responds and learns from that response. For example how many of us think about how we dress in the morning? It is so automatic that we do it without thinking. However most parents know that learning to dress is a process of stimulating the child ("now put your foot in the sock") and when the child does it correctly rewarding them ("Well done! Clever boy/girl"). In more recent study there is an acknowledgment that the brain has a mediating role in learning so, whilst the work or such people as Pavlov were referred to Stimulus – Response learning, the work of B.F. Skinner is referred to as Stimulus – Mediation – Response learning. To put this latter into context think of being hit by someone and our response. You are hit (stimulus) – You think that it hurt and why should the person get away with it (Mediation) – You hit them (Response).

The Psychoanalytical

This perspective to the study of psychology very much lies in the developments and concepts of human behaviour as described by Sigmund Freud. Most famous for his thesis on the interpretation of dreams, Freud believed that behaviour stemmed from unconscious processes. He described these under the titles the ID, the Ego and the Super Ego. The interplay between these dynamics of self create behaviour. For example, during a sermon you have the urge to go to the toilet. The Id, the primitive aspect of the self tells you to go now and have no fear of the consequences. On the other hand the Ego warns you of the spectacle you will create; the whole congregation looking at you and knowing where you are going. Arching over all this would be the Super Ego constraining your behaviour to an acceptable standard. Depending on the urgency of the situation will determine the eventual aspect that wins out and influences your behaviour.

Freud believed that we are driven by the same basic instincts as animals and that we are constantly struggling to cope with the stresses and constraints that society places on our behaviour. Where these urges are repressed heavily they need to come out in a more socially acceptable form. Hence one way of allowing these urges to come out is through dreams whilst another way is through behaviour.

The Subjective

This perspective can be found mainly in the study of social development and personality. It believes that human behaviour is a result of how we see the world and not how the world actually is. We construct ideas about the world that allow is to rationalize what we see and what we experience. Thus the study of behaviour from this perspective relies heavily on self reporting so as to be able to see how the person came to behave as they did. This will include such things as ones culture and personal history whilst also taking into account how the person is feeling at the time and their degree of motivation.

In relation to religious experience there is often seen a clear link between the perception of fear and the reality. For example, when people are fearful of death, as when going into hospital for a major operation, the need to pray and believe in a great god increases. However, the reality is that very few people die under the surgeon's knife these days in developed countries. Following the successful operation and recovery the need to pray and belief in a greater god goes away as the fear subsides.

Major Subfields of Psychology

Reader's Activity

At this point you might like to think of the different situations you have heard or experienced psychologists working in. List where they were and what the psychologist was doing

We now turn to the subfields of psychological study and the roles that psychologists play within them. Your list from above may include meeting a psychologist at the child development clinic, at school, or following some traumatic event in your life. More rarely you may well have been approached by one in the street asking for you participate in a questionnaire or small experiment. From the television or crime novel you might have included psychologist working with those showing criminal behaviour. All of these come from the perspectives we discussed earlier. Subfields are where the psychologists take the theory from a particular school and apply it to people or situations

Biological psychology mainly concentrates on experimental work looking at, as we have discussed earlier, the relationship between the brain and behaviour. Much of this work is done in universities. However some government establishments and independent research organizations also undertake such work. Sometimes this work has to be done on animals, in particular, our closest relative, the chimpanzee. The results of such work allow us to more fully understand the links between the brain and behaviour.

Developmental psychology attempt to understand the factors that affect our psychological development from the cradle to the grave. Psychologists working in this field are most commonly seen in child development clinics measuring intellectual development and language acquisition as well as looking at abnormal behaviour patterns. However, increasingly they are also being seen working in clinics for the elderly. In particular looking at therapies that assist with memory conditions and other conditions that affect the behaviour of the elderly.

Social Psychology is predominantly concerned with the behaviour of groups and social relations between and amongst people. Social psychologists study group behaviour and group dynamics. This is mainly done by observation or, on rare occasions, through social experiment. Perhaps the best know social experiment was the Milgram (1965) study on obedience. This took people from the street and asked them to teach a person to do a task. If the subject got the task wrong the teacher from the street was to give an electric shock. The more times the subject got it wrong the higher the voltage of the shock. Whilst preparing the teacher to the task the experimenter slips into the conversation that the subject has a heart condition. The teacher sees the subject being wired for the shocks and believes that when pressing the button he is actually giving a shock. In reality the subject is an actor and is not receiving any shocks at all. The result of this experiment demonstrated how obedient we were when, as in this case, our resolve faltered and we were encourager by a person we perceived to be in higher authority to undertake a task.

Clinical Psychology has the largest group of psychologists working in it. They are mainly found working in hospitals and clinical institutions providing treatment and counseling over a wide range of conditions. Primarily they work on conditions that have a behavioural or emotional component. The treatments are often in groups which concentrate on changing behaviour by group pressure. Alternatively a behaviour modification approach might be employed. Counseling is used in those conditions that are of a less serious nature and the focus is on understanding why a client feels and behaves as they do.

Educational Psychology, as its name suggests, looks at how we learn. Psychologists working in this speciality specifically concentrate on children who have learning and emotional problems and how learning and teaching strategies can be developed to overcome the child's difficulties.

Experimental Psychology whilst being a term that could be applied to all branches of psychology in this case, mainly refers to that work undertaken in behavioural and clinical psychology. The experiments undertaken often look at how humans respond to stimuli and how such stimuli affect the perception of the worlds in which we live.

Organizational Psychology could be described as one of the newer subfields looking, as it does, as to how people are selected as most suitable for particular jobs. This is often done by what is called psychometric testing; asking questions or solving puzzles that relate to how a job might be done. They are also involved in looking at how collaboration and teamwork could be developed in the workplace. This may be through design of the environment or how people react with the technology they have to use.

Contemporary Psychological Perspectives

With this great span of psychological study the need for research has never been so great as it is today. Increasingly psychologists are not only looking at their own field but also those of other disciplines such as chemistry and physiology to further their understanding of human behaviour and it's origins. Linked to this has been the development of technology that has allowed us, for the first time, to see the brain actually working. As was stated earlier, MRI scanning has allowed us to watch the brain working and allows us to map function more closely to brain anatomy.

Many of the hypothesis' that have been developed over the years have been able to be challenged in the light of this new research. Whilst it has been possible to clearly show where physical functions originate in the brain it has not yet been possible the demonstrate where thought and memory reside. MRI scanning have been unraveling this mystery. It now appears that memory closely resides to the sides where action originates from. So, for example, if you are remembering a picture, then the area in the brain responsible for sight seems to be stimulated. If you are remembering sounds then the area responsible for hearing appears to be stimulated. If one things about this it is quite a good survival strategy. For if there was only one memory centre and that was damaged by physical trauma then the whole memory could be wiped out. Attempting to identify where attitude originates from in the brain is much less clear and work is still in its very early stages to develop a hypothesis.

However, such interesting work does lead one to think about some of the mysteries associated with religious behaviour and understanding. For example one aspect of the religious is the concept of the soul. Has MRI found any area of the brain that could be the possible site of the soul? What effect does prayer and meditation have physically on the brain. Equally does spiritual healing have any effect on the body?

Psychology,Religious Belief and Health

The answer to these age old questions is being unlocked and is producing some very surprising answers. 'Some have described the findings as if God had been "hotwired" into the brain,(Benner, 2002) However the Dr Newberg , one of the leading experts in this area of study, has described this has being too radical. His studies have shown that there are changes that take place when religious activity is practiced. For example, Newberg invited local communities of monks and runs into his laboratory and injected them with radioactive tracers that allowed him to monitor any changes in blood flow to the different regions of the brain during meditation.

Newberg had hypothesized that many areas of the brain would be involved during these spiritual practices. The main areas of the brain that the team thought would be involved included the frontal lobe, which allows us to focus our attention and the parietal lobes, which help us distinguish ourselves from the outside world. The results of the experiments showed that in meditation changes in the brain activity did take place. The Frontal lobe appeared to decrease in activity whilst the Parietal lobe also decreased in activity, blocking off sensory inputs from outside and altering the sense of self. What did surprise the researchers was that the Thalamus, which plays a key roll in allowing parts of the brain to communicate with each other, showed greatly increased activity, when one would have expected it's activity to diminish.

Some believe that this shows that in creating man, God created the brain to be responsive to prayer and meditation. In his book, "Why God won't Go away" (Newberg 2001) Newberg remains open minded and steers a mid line between religion and science so as to create, as he calls it, "dialogue" What is clear is that something does happen in the brain when we pray and when we meditate and these changes appear to be beneficial to the physiological state of the body. If this is the case with prayer and meditation then what happens with spiritual healing and the laying on of hands?

Hear too modern psychological research has been unlocking a few doors. After the second world war clinical psychology became a profession that concentrated on healing. One area that was looked at was the effect of positive thought on pathologies, i.e. physical conditions. What psychologists found was that, by making people think positively about their physical disorder the effects of such disorders where reduced. In some cases the condition seemed to go into remission. This type of therapy was further developed by some clinical psychologists working with terminally ill patients. They found that by getting the patients to focus on the tumor and actively think about it reducing there appeared to be changes in the growth pattern of that tumor. The difficulty with such claims has always been how to substantiate them.

With the aid of chemists and physiologists such therapies relating to positive thought have been able to be studied. What researchers have found is that positive thinking about getting better does have physical effects. For example, a study conducted in The Bristol Homeopathic Centre in 1996 told several women to meditate daily in the idea of the tumors being attacked by white blood cells. Several of the women developed story lines that imagined soldiers of cleaners going to the tumor and attacking or cleaning it. This went on for some months. At the same time a group of other women with similar cancers were given counseling. The group that had been given the positive thought therapy achieved a far higher degree of remission in their cancer growths than the control group At the same time blood samples were taken to examine the blood chemistry. This too was found to have been affected, with raised levels of white blood cells and other positive changes to the blood morphology. What is not clear is what effect the "laying on of hands" has in spiritual healing. The key difficulty is how one can study the effects. Once this issue is resolved one can assume from what has been described above, that some interesting findings will be found

References:

Benner.D (2002) Meditation and the Brain, http://Serendip.bynmawr. Edu/bb/neuro99/web2/benner.html

Newberg.A.et al (2001) Why God Won't Go Away: Brain Science and the Biology of Belief.

Chapter 2:

PSYCHOLOGY IN RELIGION

The Contribution of Psychology to the Study of Religion

The relationship between psychology and religion has, for many years, been quite ambivalent. However, over the past few years, this attitude has been changing. There has been an increasing realization that religious belief and practice do have an effect on us and our behaviour. In the last chapter we started to see some of the physical effects that belief and practice have on the brain but there is a greater realization that some form of belief in a spiritual realm of life is essential to a healthy well being (Koenig et al 1997). Even expressing a non belief in some form of spiritual life is in fact a form of belief.

Reader's Activity

Think about the religious people you have met and see if the way they express their religious beliefs matches their personality. Make a list of the different ways people express their religiosity.

Religious belief affects our thoughts and feelings in and to every day life. If we reflect on the various personality types that one meets in any religion one can see how their belief affects their understanding of life. Their personality type will also affect the type of religion they will practice. Byrnes (1984) states that there are three key personality types that one sees in religious practice. The first he calls the "Healthy – Minded". These people rejoice in everybody and everything and feel, according to Byrne, "grateful admiration for the gift of so happy an existence". All life is a joy and, as a consequence their faith and belief is also a joy. Thus, they need a religious practice that is joyful extravert and very social. Not for them the idea of meditation in solitude, reflection and quiet prayer.

The second group identified by Byrnes are the "Sick Souls". These individuals often see life as a morbid existence in a world full of sin and evil. They believe that we live in a sin sick world and that, come judgment day, retribution will be delivered to the sinful and the pure in heart will triumph. Such people, according to Byrnes, are of the "persuasion that the evil aspects of life are at its very essence, and that the world's meaning mostly comes home when we take religious teaching to heart". Such a gloomy existence on life can cause pathological melancholy is some people. The French psychologist Ribort called this *Anhedonia*. It is hardly likely then that such people would go and join a "Happy – Clappy" form of religious practice. It is far more likely that they will belong to a belief system that emphasizes judgment and retribution for wrong doing. In the system of religions these tend to be fundamentalist in their approach and very strict in their belief and religious adherence. In so doing it fulfils a need in such individuals. There are quite a few examples of such people in History. Classic, perhaps, is John Bunyan who in much of his writing saw himself as the great sinner and looking forwards to a life hereafter free from sin.

The three types outlined by Byrnes are the "Twice Born". These are people who have been living a life free from religious constraints or, indeed, in some cases, opposed to forms of religion. Then at some point, often through some event in life, they undergo a conversion experience that changes their outlook on life. They become "saved" and a new order comes to their life. They are "Born Again" The Christian religion is full of such examples, St. Paul on the Damascus Road, St Augustine of Hippo; who lives a debauched life until he saw Jesus. Often it is found that such people whilst living a life free from religious conviction, have had a questing or unease about how there are currently living their lives. They often describe life as "lacking meaning" and having "no purpose". The religion they join gives meaning to that existence and often reflect their personality type. We shall look at this in more detail in later chapters. However we need to look in a little more detail at the whole idea of conversion.

Conversion can be described as a self surrender to a belief that gives meaning to existence to life and hope for the future. Often it is the reunification of a divided self; energies are first directed one way, i.e. full of life excesses and then another, i.e. a realization that such a life is wrong. The most often reported are as those outlines above, dramatic, sudden and instant life saving. However conversion can also be willed by people. They gradually build up new ideas and discard the old ones and, in so doing, developing a firm set of religious belief and ways to live. As we shall see later, this phenomenon has been studied by some of the most eminent names in psychology with some interesting conclusions.

Looking at these religious types one thing becomes increasingly clear and that is the need for some sort of code that defines what is good and what is evil. These codes often relate to behaviour in the self and also in society. For without a moral code to live by life would be anarchy. Thus from earliest times we find that belief systems laid down codes for people to live by. One of the earliest examples is that of the Ten Commandments which not only lays down the relationship for the Israelites with their God but also how they should live one with another in their community. In so doing an ordered existence could be established that would give safety and security to members of the community whilst, at the same time, allowing them to live the religious life.

Following such a code defines behaviour as being good, whilst deviation could be described as evil, often because it is harmful and detrimental to society. This then allows individuals to make judgments on their own and other's behaviour. Where such behaviour is seen as being extreme then retribution by the group can be exacted and the deviant corrected and brought back into line. Without such codes of behaviour it would be impossible to mediate behaviour and get people to conform. Without this there would be a total breakdown in society, law and order. Some people believe that Britain is in a post Christian era and, with the demise of the faith, has come the demise of social behaviour and, as a consequence we have a breakdown in law and order i.e. there is a rise in anti social behaviour.

Integrating Psychology into the Understanding of the Religious Experience

Whilst the need for a moral code of behaviour might be quite clear what is not so well understood is the need for the idea of some form of life after death, yet this concept forms the backbone of much of religious thinking and belief. There is a famous saying that there are only two things sure in this life, death and taxes. Death is often the last thing that we talk about and yet it is the surest thing that will happen to us. The reason for this compartmentalization of the subject is that we fear death. This is reflected in the way that we treat the dead. In most religions the dead body is seen as unclean and untouchable and some rite of purification is needed to be performed. The grave also is seen as a place of darkness and evil. It is for this reason that one finds tombstones or gravel capping the grave so as to keep the evil buried.

When asking people to describe the experience of death they often define it as something singular and lonely. People are frightened of dying alone. This then has a knock on effect about where people want to die. In the United Kingdom about half of all deaths take place in hospital or nursing homes. By their very nature these are seen to be lonely places to die what with monitor, drips and the like around the dying person. Most people, when asked, would prefer to die at home with their family and friends around them.

Whilst most people talk about the fear of dying, when it comes to thoughts of what happens after death there is a far greater diversity of thinking. Whilst some have a belief in an afterlife, others believe in there being nothing at all. In years past there has been speculation that holding a belief in there being nothing after death could have a detrimental effect of our mental well being. In recent years some of this speculation has been confirmed by research. Oman & Reed (1998) have conducted quite a few longitudinal studies into states of physical and mental health between those with a belief in the "Hereafter" and those without. These studies, conducted over many years, have found that religious people are happier and healthier than non religious people. Actively religious people show lower mortality rates from a variety of diseases than non religious people.

Such findings are also reflected in the links between mental health and religious belief. In time past it was thought the holding strong religious belief was bad for ones mental health. This was mainly because religious belief produced feelings of guilt when one did not live up to the standards that the religious code set. The increasing body of good unbiased research into links between religious belief and mental health has found that holding a belief in the afterlife reduces panic attacks and anxiety, particularly when these are as a result of the fear of death.

The two key issues that come from death are the thoughts of

loneliness and darkness and the need of some form of continuation of life after death that gives meaning to our life here on earth. It is not surprising then to see religious writers and philosophers addressing these issues. For example the author Charles Kingsley wrote about death and the afterlife, "It is not darkness you are going to, for God is light, it is not lonely, for God is with you, it is not an unknown country, for Christ is there". All religious belief attempts to create out of death a feeling of hope. Some religions have a recycling idea about the future; depending on how well you lived in this live will determine how you return and in what body. Whilst others see the afterlife as some form of utopia where only the good will be admitted, whilst the bad perish. Such beliefs appear to affect our mental and physical health and well being

Another religious concept that has a psychological significance is that of saintliness. From a religious perspective saintliness is the ultimate in personality development In Religious terms it is when the individual comes closest to matching the ideal. Many psychological theorists, whilst not using the term saintliness have talked about achieving a state of self fulfillment or "self actualization" as in Maslow's hierarchy of needs. The result of this is often seen as an inner calm and a sense of love and good will to the world. From this inner calm comes a conviction and determination to do what is right, often at the cost of self even to death. Such people become examples of how to live to others who follow the faith. At this point, especially in this day post 9-11 we need to make a division between saintliness and martyrdom. Martyrdom is often used when a person is killed for what they believe and, as a consequence become heroes of the faith. Often, martyrdom gives specific privileges to the individual. For example they may gain rapid access to the afterlife. It may also mean that all their former sins are forgiven without judgment. A martyr is not automatically called a saint.

As part of our human condition we all need people to look up to and roll models to follow. Whilst in the past this was the roll of the saints, today it is the roll of the pop idol or fashion guru. Note how religious words such as "idol" and "guru" are used to describe these rolls. They are people that, particularly the young look up to and follow but, as so often, they are found to be plaster saints with not substance or experience.

Religious Experience from the Psychological Perspective

Byrnes, (1984) in his book on psychology and religion describes religion as a mystical experience which has its roots in consciousness. He describes three attributes of this mystical state. Firstly Ineffability. The experience cannot be easily described and no summary of what it might be meets the experience that most people have. It is only when one meets with another person who has had a similar experience that one can share the experience and perceive it's reality to the individuals. Quite often when people try to write about their belief they talks about "unspoken truths" or feeling of total feebleness of words in expressing what they feel.

Secondly Transiency. These mystical states brought on by religious fervor are brief and quickly pass. Otherwise they would cease to be distinctive from other emotions in normal life and, therefore, lose their power. They are so powerful in the individual that they cannot be sustained for long. Often writers talk about the feeling of "walking with God" of being filled inwardly with such joy and peace, a peace that the world cannot give.

Thirdly, Passivity. The mystical state seems to come on of its own accord. It cannot be caused in any absolute way or hurried. It can be encouraged by preparation such as meditation or the performance of a physical task but, in the main people who have a religious experience talk about a powerlessness of their will to cause the feelings to happen.

Whilst it is true that these mystical experiences are mainly found in the lives of the religious, they are not exclusive. They can also be found when listening to music or reading poetry. Often they inspire deep insights and thoughts that have a profound effect on the individual. But how do we explain them away? It is here that psychology allows us to more fully understand the behaviour that the individual is experiencing.

Whilst awake, or in the conscious state the brain is actively monitoring ourselves and the environment in which we are moving so as to remember and control our behaviour and to respond to the environment and the stimuli in it. Consciousness is an active process and, as such, we have some control over it. Part of that control is to block off some part of that stimuli. Psychologists call this, altering the state of consciousness. Often this is achieved by mental functioning being superior to physical functioning. For example, if one is sitting down, one has to worry less about dangers one might encounter such as walking and think more. Prolonged thinking often reduces the perception of stimuli from the outside environment. One becomes more focused on the thoughts that one is having. In so doing physical function increasingly shuts down until it is similar to that found in normal sleep patterns. Indeed, one study (Younger et al 1975) in which EEG readings were recorded whilst the individuals were meditating showed that most spent a large part of their time in psychological sleep. Thus, in the mystical religious experience the individual is often in a state of waking sleep, a state that allows for the development of dreams.

Reader's Activity

Think about the way you pray. Make a list of the different types of prayer you use and in what situations you have used them.

Write a few words on what are the effects of prayer for you

Most religions have some element of prayer, i.e. where the individual speaks in some way to the God of their belief. Prayer requires the individual to believe that a) they have the ability to commune with their God and b) that this God listens and has the ability to respond. Again Byrnes describes elements to the devotional experience. Unlike the mystical experience the devotional experience can be described because of the fact that prayer has to be communicated. Therefore the experience is Describable, "I told God....". Equally some people say they hear God talking to them, "He told me....".

Secondly, unlike the mystical experience, during the devotional experience the individual is in complete control of their consciousness. Byrnes calls this a Noetic State, where the individual is not transformed by some force outside of themselves over which they have no control. They are able to analyze the mental and emotional contents of the experience. Thirdly, the experience is not transient and fleeting, but long term and frequent. There is no great intensity to the experience, no dreamlike state, but just a feeling of communicating in a very intimate way with a friend or confidant. Lastly the experience is an active experience. Namely one has to get and do it. It is taught and in many people becomes a habit; saying prayers at fixed points in the day. People often talk about the power of prayer and its influence on individuals but does prayer actually have any effect?

In the previous chapter we discussed an outline of the physical effects meditation and prayer has on the brain. Whilst this described changes observed in the brain it does not explain why people pray and the benefits they receive from it. For many prayer allows the individual to share with their God the concerns, worries and fears that they have. Few people actually pray in any great depth thanking God or expressing joy. Most people pray when there is a crisis in their lives. As a consequence it can be seen as a coping mechanism to deal with anxiety and stress

Psychologists have long studied the ways that people cope with stress. Several strategies have been observed that have some relationship to prayer. In most strategies the first step is to clearly define the problem. By taking time out and sitting or kneeling this often allows the individual to focus on what the problem actually is. From that point the individual has possible solutions. These could be changes to the environment, other or indeed within one's self. Psychologist call this the Problem – Focused Coping strategy. According to Billings & Moos (1984) people who use this strategy are often found to have lower levels of depressions during and after stressful situations. In studying people who use this strategy one key element is the chance to talk the possible solutions through with a confidant. This is what prayer allows the individual to do.

Another strategy is to engage in focusing on the emotions created by anxiety and stress so as to stop them overwhelming the individual. This strategy can be divided into two types of displacement behaviors. The first is physical, where the individual may engage in physical activity to lessen the stress, i.e. positively by taking part in physical exercise or negatively by drinking excessively or taking drugs. The second is by indulging in cognitive activity (thinking) which helps to reduce the threat. For example, by placing the situation into God hands, believers often talk about a feeling of relief and calmness. In fact what they have done is to "displace" the problem from their shoulders to that of God. Another strategy is to ascribe the fault for the problem causing the stress not to oneself but to another. In some cases this could be God. This "attribution" approach also allows the individual to cope by allowing them to think the cause was not their fault but someone else's.

In these strategies Levy (1990) found that people who found emotional support from others seemed to cope better with stress. In a study of women with breast cancer Levy found that women who had social support had a higher immune response to cancer cells than those who coped alone. One area where people got support was from the church and prayer groups. Levy noted that churches regularly called for these women to be remembered in prayer and also prayed with the women, asking for God to help and support them in their fight against cancer. Some churches even had healing services where the minister placed hands on the individual and prayed over them as part of Sunday worship.

From this and other studies it has been found that prayer plays an important psychological role in allowing us to cope with the strains and stresses of everyday life. How it works is by giving us ritual, structure and certainty at times when life is uncertain and full of unknowns. Prayer also gives us an avenue to vent feelings. Thus, one finds that the conversations or exchanges between our Gods run the full gamut from calm sense that one is being listened to, through rage and anger for being done to, to the sense that one is being responded to.

Some researchers also point to the fact that for prayer to work, the individual has to have an active imagination. This is deemed to be essential. For the individual needs to be able to imagine the god they are talking to. This is similar to the focused problem solving we talked about earlier. Some people, when praying, talk about seeing God and imagining Him talking to them and even performing healing acts. Some work has shown that such imaginings actually help the individual in coping with what ever stress they are under.

All of this seems to be linked with levels of consciousness. We have already broached the subject of what happens to our conscious when we pray and meditate but this raises the question as to whether it is possible to lift the state of consciousness to a "higher plain". Many religions that use meditation as the basis of religious contemplation have people who become so deeply focused on thought that they are able to block out all harmful stimuli. They are able to tolerate extremes of pain that in their normal condition they would be unable to stand. Research into this is still in its initial stages, but here again EEG readings and MRI scans have shown that the individual has the ability to control the receptors and their sensitivity to outside stimuli. In other words we could have more control over our body and minds that first thought.

What all this points to is that an understanding of psychology can help in the understanding of why humans need religion and the effects that this has on our lives. Newburg states that if we did not already have religions in the world we would have to invent them to fulfill a human need. This can be born out by looking at anthropology studies which demonstrate that in all human settlements across all the world there has some form of god worship. Religion is fundamental to human behaviour and the control of it fundamental to religion

References:

Koenig .H.G. et al.(1997) Modeling the cross section relationships between religion, physical health, social support and depressive symptoms, American Journal of Geriatric Psychology5, 131-144

Byrnes J.F.(1984) The Psychology of Religion, The Free Press, New York

Ribot.T Younger.J, et. Al.(1975) Sleep during transcendental meditation, Perceptual and Motor Skills. 40. 1325-1330

Levy.S, et al(1990) Perceptual Social Support and tumor estrogen/ progesterone receptor status as predictors of natural killer cell activity in breast cancer patients. Psychosomatic Medicine, 52. 78-85

Chapter 3:

PERSONALITY DEVELOPMENT AND RELIGION

What is Personality?

At the beginning of the book we talked about psychology being the science that everyone thought they knew something about but, in fact, know very little. Personality is one of the subjects that demonstrates this most clearly. We often talk about people's personality and interchange it with other words such a character and temperament thinking that they are synonyms for the same thing whereas, in fact, they are not. Personality also gets linked with the way people behave, i.e. "he has a violent personality". Whilst Personality, character and temperament are linked, they not the same thing. So what is Personality? According to the 14th Edition of Atkinsons, Introduction to Psychology" (2003) Personality can be defined as:

> ***The distinctive and characteristic patterns of thought, emotion and Behaviour that make up an individual's personal style of interacting with the physical and social environment.***

In other words it is the sum total of the way you think, feel and behave to the people and surroundings in which we live and operate. So what do we mean by *character and temperament?* In years past children leaving school use to be given a character reference. This described the individual's traits and behaviour. For example the reference would talk about the person being honest, trustworthy a good timekeeper etc. All of these point to the way that the person behaved. That is what is meant by character; the way that the individual tends to behave in given situations. Temperament, on the other hand mainly refers to a persons disposition, .i.e. their mood. "This person had quite a placid nature". Whilst quite clearly these two elements can be seen as parts of what we call personality they are not, in their own entity, substitutes for it.

In trying to study Personality, psychologists have devised a whole series of theories as to how it develops and, indeed and have long argued as to whether it is something that is inborn (innate) or something we develop as a reaction to our environment whilst growing up. The truth of the matter is that, whilst theories go some way to explain what personality is, not one theory offers a complete answer to the questions outlined above.

In the earliest studies of Personality psychologists relied on everyday language to help define what elements made up our personality. They called these elements traits, meaning a feature of behaviour. Allport & Odbert (1936) resorted to looking in the dictionary to find words that described, in their view, traits of behaviour. In this laborious study they found nearly 18.000 words that described some trait of personality. This was, quite obviously, an unmanageable amount of traits to make into a cogent theory. By removing synonyms and obscure words they were able to reduce the list but it was not until 1957 that Cattell brought this down to 200 traits that could be used to define personality. These included such traits as, openness, agreeability and sociable.

Long before the development of trait theory some people, such as Freud, had attempted to define personality without resorting to the use of traits. To explain how personality influenced the individual they developed new words, such as the Id or Ego, words that have become common in the English language.

Theories of Personality

The Psychoanalytic Approach

At the outset it is important to state that this theory, of all the theories of personality, is the least scientific, and yet remains one of the most influential. Based on the work of Freud it relies for its basis not on scientific fact but on his observations whilst working as a neurologist and treating patients with nervous diseases. From his observations and by talking to patients he was able to identify thought patterns that seemed to go with certain types of behaviour. He also found that thoughts and themes discussed by the patients often were also revealed in dreams. From this Freud developed the theory that our personality was a manifestation of subconscious thoughts and fears.

In his book "The Psychopathology of Everyday Life" (1901) he argued that such things as dreams, forgetting and slips of the tongue were manifestations of these subconscious processes. This was a way in which repressed thoughts and fears came to the conscious world. From his observations he developed what he called the "iceberg" model of the mind. Much of what goes on in our mind is below the surface, like an iceberg, and only small glimpses of it appear above the surface. However he found that this idea was too simplistic and went on to develop a structural model which divided personality into three major elements that interacted together and governed our personality. He called these three elements the Id, Ego and Superego.

The Id, according to Freud, was the most primitive of the three elements and was what we were born with. The Id was made up of our most basic drives, such as the need for food, drink, sleep and the avoidance of pain. There was also a drive for self preservation which manifested itself in the drives of aggression and the need for sex. According to Freud the Id demands immediate gratification once the drive has developed. When the drive is not satisfied then aggression comes to the fore so as to achieve gratification. Perhaps the best way to view the Id is to think of a young baby who is hungry. The child feels the pangs of hunger and demands gratification. To get that gratification the child cries at a pitch that causes discomfort to the hearing of the carer. The carer brings food to the child and the child eats the crying stops. If the child were not to be fed immediately then the crying would become more intense and cause such annoyance that the only way to cause the crying to stop would be to feed the child. In modern parlance this is often referred to as the "pleasure principle", seeking satisfaction without thinking of the consequences.

The Ego develops from the Id. Carers soon teach the child that immediate gratification of one's needs is not the way of the world. There is an old saying that to "Spare the rod spoils the child". This period of time is often quite demanding of both child and carer. The child attempts to seek gratification whilst the carer seeks to impose rules on to the child behaviour. These periods of conflict have passed into poplar culture at "The Terrible Two's" and the like. It is when the demands of the Id have to subject to the realities of the environment in which the child lives. It is not always possible to have food on demand, emptying ones bladder has to take place in certain places and aggression is not a tolerable way to behave. All of the social norms have to be learnt. It is the reality of the world in which we live. Thus, if the Id obeys the Pleasure Principle then the Ego obeys the "Reality Principle". The Ego governs the Id and determines what drives are to be met and in what manner. It also looks at how the satisfaction will take place, to ensure that it is socially acceptable. In other words it makes us sociable

The Superego is the arbiter between the Id and the Ego. It judges the needs of the Id and the response of the Ego as to whether the action was right or wrong. It is the repository of a moral and social conscience as well as our ideal self. It develops as a response to the rewards and punishments that our carers impose upon us during our upbringing. Thus it is very much influenced by our parents' culture and religion. Whilst as children we have carers, parents teachers etc. to tell us what is right or wrong by adulthood it is the Superego that serves this function. Violating the standards set by the Superego causes within us anxiety and fear. Depending on how well the superego is developed will depend our degree of moral and social behaviour. Those who commit persistent antisocial acts could be deemed to have a poorly developed superego whilst those who show a high degree of conscience and socially acceptable behaviour are well developed superegos.

According to Freud these three elements are in constant interplay. Whist the Id demands gratification the Ego is trying to find socially acceptable forms of gratification and above these two sits the superego constantly battling with the other two because the behaviour often falls short of what is ideal. In the well balanced individual the interplay between these three is socially acceptable whilst the unbalanced of has the Id in the ascendancy.

The interplay between these three produces what some call, psychic energy, or drives. As was said earlier these drives have to be satisfied to achieve drive reduction. If they cannot be satisfied in acceptable ways then other means need to be found. Such behaviors often appear to be satisfied in a disguised form for example, through dreams or alternative behaviors. However, the urge to do something that is socially unacceptable causes anxiety to build up in the individual. These anxieties have to be reduced, just live drives. As a consequence we develop mechanisms that allow us to cope with these anxieties; they are called Mental Defense Mechanisms.

Mental Defense Mechanisms

Freud and his daughter Anna defined these Mental Defense Mechanisms as strategies for preventing or reducing anxiety. They defined seven mechanisms in all and we use all of these defense mechanisms at one time or another in our lives. They help us to cope with the difficult and stressful events in our lives more directly. However, at times they can become too dominant and, as a consequence, cause to develop maladaptive behaviour. These Mental Defense Mechanisms are as follows:-

Denial

This is when we deny that an event has taken place. Often these events are unpleasant or emotionally traumatic and as a consequence they are so repressed as to be almost forgotten. In a milder form the individual tends to reduce the degree of harm that the event has caused. It is sometimes found in cases of abuse that the abuser or the abused deny the event taking place or ask what harm such a small event could have on the individual.

Rationalization

Here the individual attempts to explain away the events that have taken place in a more rational form. In working with convicted child sex offenders I often found that the offenders talked about what they did in the guise of sex education and warning children as to what other people could do to harm them. In searching for a good reason rather than the true reason, the individual is making an excuse.

Repression

This is when impulses or memories are too frightening or painful to cope with and, as a consequence, they are totally excluded from our conscious awareness. Memories that evoke shame, guilt or self deprecation are the ones most commonly repress is the thought of death. Repression is a subconscious activity and, as such is different from suppression which is a conscious activity. In suppression the individual controls the activity. Freud believed that repression is seldom successful and, as a result, impulses or thoughts break through into the conscious through a slip of the tongue.

Projection

How often have you had someone talk about what they see as your faults only for you to think that they are actually describing themselves? This is in fact a defense mechanism called projection. What we recognized as our own undesirable qualities are assigned to other people in exaggerated accounts.

Reaction Formation

Is perhaps the most difficult of all the Mental Defense Mechanisms to understand. Suppose a mother really does not love her child. She hides the feeling she had by demonstrating the opposite reaction. She may show distress when the child is away from her. She may become overindulgent to the child or take the child's wishes and implement them in an extreme form. For example, suppose the child expresses a wish to play tennis, rather than just buying some balls and a racket, the mother goes the whole hog and purchases lessons from a coach and enrolls the child in the local club. In fact under the guise of being kind the parent is in fact being very controlling and cruel to the child. Whilst the above example relates to a child this happens in quite a few adult situations and relationships as well.

Intellectualization

This allows the individual to detach themselves from the stressful situation and form an abstract theory as to why the stressful event took place. For many who become involved in situations of human misery this mechanism is essential. For example aid workers need to become detached from the people that they are helping if they are to function competently. Failure to do so causes distress

Displacement

This mechanism allows for a drive to be directed in a different form so as to allow it's fulfillment to be socially acceptable. For example a woman who has a strong maternal instinct but is unable to have children may direct that drive in another way. This could be through having animals or by helping over humans in such occupations as nursing. Whilst this activity may not cause the drive to be fully reduced is doe help in reducing the frustration that the individual might feel.

Readers Activity

After reading the descriptions of these mental defense mechanisms think about your own life and behaviour and see if you can identify any of these mechanisms active in your own behaviour

Freud's Theory of Personality Development

Much of Freud's work led him develop a stage theory to Personality Development. During each stage the pleasure seeking principle of the Id focused on different parts of the body and activities associated with it. In the first year of life infants get pleasure from oral experiences such as feeding or sucking things in their mouth. In the Second year the focus seems to change to the pleasure in excreting or withholding faeces. Around the third year until the sixth the child becomes preoccupied with the genital region. The child gains great pleasure from fondling the genitals. The child also learns to differentiate from the sexes and becomes aware of sexual impulses.

Around the age of 6 these sexual impulses in a male child tend to be directed towards their mother. The child sees the father and other male children as rival for the mother's affection. This is termed the Oedipus Conflict stage, after the Greek legend of Oedipus. Resolution of this conflict comes when the child takes the father as a role model and develops iconic attitudes towards him. Around the age of 7 to 12 the child becomes less concerned about their sexuality and more about the world in which they live and the skills needed to survive. This is called the latency stage the final stage happens is adolescences when a mature attitude to sexuality is developing and is called the genital stage.

Freud believed that if problems developed at any of these stages then it would affect our development and we would become fixated about that stage. For example if we were weaned too early we could become fixated at the oral stage. This would then show itself by us gaining pleasure by oral experiences, such a eating or sucking. People fixated at the Anal stage tend to demonstrate high degrees of orderliness and cleanliness.

In later years Freud's theories have been modified by such notable thinkers as Carl Jung. Jung added to Freud's thinking of the unconscious by describing a thing called the collective unconscious which was common to all humans. This collective unconscious consists of primordial images or archetypes inherited from our ancestors. These image or archetypes include such images of what a mother or father is and what we mean by love or death. Another person who developed Freud's theory was Harry Sack Sullivan who took the theory of psychoanalysis and from it came to the conclusion that our concept of self and others came about as a response to our experiences with others in our environment.

What ever we feel about Freud's theory of Personality his work on it established him as one of the great figures on Psychology and science of the 20th century. However, his theory of personality and it's development does offer us one of the most complete theories taking in, as it does, both innate and environmental factors of development.

The Behaviorist Approach

This approach, on the other hand, sees the new born baby as having no real personality at birth. The theory places great emphasis on the importance of how the environment, including people and events, mould and determine behaviour from the first day of our lives. In our opening chapters we talked about how behaviour could be conditioned, i.e. how reward and punishment shape our behaviour. Behaviorists believe that personality differences can be accounted for by the different ways in which we have learnt to respond to given situations. They are conditioned responses. These responses are either learned from our own experience or through our observations of others in given situations. For example seeing a person being punished for a misdemeanors will be remembered and stop us from doing the same behaviour. This approach concentrates on the process of personality development rather than the differences that we show. In so doing it shows that our personality is shaped by the unique reinforcement history that we have gone through in our formative years.

Thus, our personality depends very much upon the environment in which we were brought up in and developed. This approach has been heavily criticized for concentrating too much on the influence of social settings in shaping behaviour (Carlson 1971). However, the application of behaviorist principles to a whole range of psychological concepts has allowed theorists to re examine their thinking in relation to the interactions between people and situations. Much of this theory rests on the work of Pavlov and B.F. Skinner.

The Cognitive Approach

The cognitive approach has developed out of the behaviorist theory and, unlike the behaviorist, is in fact not a theory at all. According to Smith et al (2003) it is a general empirical approach to a set of topics that relate to how we process information about ourselves, others and the world around us. Cognitive theorists believe that individual personality differences can be explained by the way that individuals process and respond to information and the mental representations that that one makes from it.

Whilst the behaviorist saw personality as if it were a piece of clay that could be molded by out influences, with the clay doing very little to influence it's own shape; the cognitive approach sees the importance of these influences from outside but also acknowledges that thought and thought processes must have an effect as well. As humans we think. One of the great exponents of this theory was Albert Bandura and he emphasized the role of thinking in his book Social Foundations of Thought and Action. He said,

"The *process of survival would be slim... if we depended on trial and error. One doesnot teach a child to swim, an adolescent to drive and automobile by (trial and error).*

Thought plays a great part in how we behave. Bandura coined the concept of forethought, thinking about what we will do before doing it. This means that we take in possible outcomes and measure the likelihood of them happening. If these are regular behaviors then the need to think about them is less and they become automatic responses. In adult life none of us have to think about the process of dressing. What we were though, is shaped by the reinforcement we get from others and how we feel to how we look.

It becomes clear that, in comparison with other theories this approach, whilst having some merit also has some weaknesses. Whilst stating that it bases its findings on empirical research the elements that are being research are quire vague. If the information processing is individual how can this be compared to others? If the concept relies on individual social history how can it be measures and the applied to others? However, research in this area has shown that in shaping personality how we perceive ourselves and related that perception to the environment in which we operate has the greatest influence on our personality.

The Humanist Approach

As a reaction to psychoanalytical theory, which held sway for almost the first half of the 20th century some psychologists, notably Carl Rogers, developed a third approach to the study of personality. They believed that it was the subjective experiences of our life that shaped who we were and who we become. It is the sum total of our human experience that makes us who we are. Underlying all of this is our basic human needs that drive us to achieve. Rogers saw in the clients that he treated that there was always the need to go forward, develop and grow as though there was some ultimate goal that needed to be achieved. He believed that all humans had a good idea of who they were and what they could achieve and also some idea of who they would like to be and what they would like to achieve.

He called this the concept of SELF. The Self concept included all the perceptions, values and attitudes that characterize "me" or "I". Who I am and what I think I can do will influence my attitudes and behaviour in the world in which I live. The individual thus evaluates the experiences they undergo in the light of who they think they are. This then influences the way in which we behave in given situations. This is what Rogers called our "Actual Self".

From who we think we are develops the idea of who we would like to be. This Rogers referred to as the "Ideal Self". This should not be confused with the sort of question that is sometimes asked at interviews namely, "Where would you like to be in 10 years time". This is much more fundamental and is about the person you would like to be. This ideal self may have no foundation in reality but does give the individual something to aim for and to achieve.

Rogers believed that the closer these two concepts of Self were the happier and more stable the person would be. The further apart they were the more imbalanced and disturbed the individual would be. When the actual and ideal were the same, almost impossibility, then we would have achieved "Self Actualization" or self fulfillment.

From this it becomes clear that what is key in shaping personality is not so much, the environment or the interplay between the conscious and unconscious but the way that we define our role in the world and what we believe our destiny to be. Humanistic psychologists believe that our psychological well being depends on this need to self actualize and to be constantly moving forward to new goals. In truth self actualization is almost impossible to achieve because once we near the goals we seem to set new goals. Thus self actualization is a fleeting and transient experience.

Overlapping the work of Rogers was that of Abraham Maslow who also was working on how need fulfillment affected our behaviour. Maslow is best known for the development of a hierarchy of human needs. This hierarchy, according to Maslow, started off with a set of basic physiological needs, hunger, thirst etc. Maslow believed

needs at one level need to be partially achieved before those at another level become important motivators for our actions. However, whilst advancing through hierarchy should a lower level of need become less satisfied then our needs drop to that level. For example, in most developed countries the majority of the population will be functioning at quite a high level in the hierarchy. Should war or famine strike the land and food become short and people feel insecure then the need to find security and food will become paramount. Only when these basic needs are secure again will they start to rise through the hierarchy.

At the highest point of this hierarchy of needs is the concept of self actualization. This can only be achieved when all the other needs have been satisfied. For him these were people who had fully achieved their potential. He studied the lives of high achievers from history, such as Lincoln, Einstein and many of the US Presidents. From this he was able to distinguish characteristics of self actualizes. Things such as accepting people and situations for what they are, having a realistic view of life and the ability to laugh seemed important. Along with these characteristics he also identified behaviors that lead one to self actualize. Such things as wanting to try new things, being honest and having the ability to assume responsibility appeared to be important. Later in his studies, like Rogers, Maslow found that the nearer one got to self actualization the more balanced and healthy the individual became.

The Evolutionary Approach

This is the "the new kid on the block" as far as personality theory is concerned but, as the name suggests has it's origins in the work of the evolutionists of the 19th century. Darwin's evolutionary theory was that anything that increases the chances of survival is adopted by species so as to increase chances of growth of a species. This approach formed the basis of the work of Wilson (1975). He believed that personality was made up of behaviors, selected over evolutionary history, that increase the chances of surviving and leaving descendants. Much of the research in Evolutionary Psychology has been around the personality behaviors that seem to be most successful in choosing mates.

In some ways this theory attempts to address many of the questions that are age old in relation to the differences in the sexes. It has long been recognized that what women look for in a mate is different to that of a male. Females invest a large part of their time to the rearing of children and the provision of a safe and secure environment for the family to live in. Thus, she will look for a mate that will provide genes that will produce strong health children and also have the ability to provide for the family and share in the child rearing. Men on the other hand look primarily for females that are available, willing and fertile. Other attributes come well down the line.

This view in the 21st century is obviously not politically too correct but, over our evolutionary history, this has been the case. Some interesting research over the past few years has shown that whilst we might not like this view of things we still behave in ways to meet these aims. For example much of female fashion is about making one look young. Wearing high heals, makes the leg look juvenile; anti aging creams attempt to take wrinkles away. In emphasizing youth and beauty the females is attempting to show fertility to any potential mate. Males, on the other hand, tend to demonstrate strength and wealth to potential mates. This is done by being a flashy dressers and spending money, and when challenged, being able to hold ones own in a fight, be that physical or mental. Thus, the behaviors that we each learn that makes us successful with the opposite sex become part of our personality behaviors (Buss 1996).

A proxy for fertility is youth whilst a proxy for wealth could be age. This could explain why older men become attractive to younger women. These sexual preferences have been found in a wide variety of cultures (Buss 1989). They can even be spotted in singles ads in any newspaper. Just look at the ages for which interest has been expressed. Women look for older males whilst males look for younger women However, to think that this theory is just about mating would do it an injustice. People such as Gray (1992) and Tanner (1990) have demonstrated that the need for survival and successful reproduction has broader implications for the personality differences found between the sexes. Men, if they are to be successful providers and mates have to be more focused and individualistic than females. If there is competition then having the ability to problem solve and be dominant will increase the chances of the male winning over another. Females on the other hand, need good inter social skills. If she is to bring up her brood successfully then the ability to get along with others and share as well as being good communicators become very important.

This starts to become more interesting when competition for mating partners becomes more intense. In some developed countries with a declining birth rate females have started to outnumber males. This is quite a unique situation because males have always been in the majority throughout evolutionary history. With this change in the demographic structure there has also been a change in the behaviour of females and males. Whilst aggression in young male adults was quite common this was not the case in females. However, over the past decade the number of violent offences committed by young women has increased alarmingly. Some evolutionary psychologists believe that this could be because of the increased competition for male mates. Males, on the other hand, need to fight less for female mates and, as a consequence seem to be thinking more about appearance. In recent years we have seen fashion trends where men wear earrings, eye makeup and more flamboyant clothing; once the preserve of females.

Is it any wonder then that this theory has taken quite a deal of flack from a whole variety of groups who see this as sexist and politically incorrect? But to dismiss it out of hand would be to do a great injustice to some interesting work. Evolutionary theory does give some powerful arguments to a whole range of behaviors and new explanations to some old questions. Whilst still quite a new theory, it's body of research evidence is growing quite prolifically and will be able to answer some of its critics in the years to come.

Trait Theory

At the beginning of this chapter we talked about characteristics are Traits of personality that could be identified in the behaviour of individuals. Over the years various psychologists narrowed these factors down from thousands to hundreds. It wasn't until the work of Eysenck (1953) that these traits were put into some meaningful theory. Through factor analysis he arrived at two personality traits, introvert-extravert and emotional stability-instability.

Introvert – Extravert refers to the degree to which and individual is orientated inward towards themselves or outward towards the world. At the introvert end of the scale the person is shy, withdrawn and likes solitude, whilst at the extravert end of the scale the individual is out going, sociable and needing company. The dimensions of stable – unstable relate to the emotionality of the individual. According to Eysenck we all sit somewhere in the paradigms set by these two axes. In the main the more introverted we are the more emotionally unable we become and vice versa.

Much of Eysenck's work has now passed into the popular vocabulary and the tests for personality that he developed are used quite widely. However, what has not really been resolved is the actual numbers of traits there really are. In the last decade a consensus has been emerging. Through the work of such people as Ozer (1994) and McCrae (1999) it appears that five trait dimensions seem to capture what we mean by personality. The Big Five as they have become know are Openness, Conscientiousness, Extraversion, Agreeableness and Neuroticism. According to Smith (2003) many personality psychologists consider the discovery of the Big Five to be the major breakthrough of contemporary psychology. How they will develop and he used in understanding personality remains to be seen.

How religious belief plays a part in personality development

Readers Activity

After reading these various theories of personality and it's development think about a theory that you find most appealing and seek if you can identify how having a religious believe could play a part in the development of personality. You might like to write some conclusions down.

In looking at all these theories of personality and its development what becomes very clear is that is not something that is totally innate. For personality to develop there has to be some reaction with other people. The prime people involved are the parents or carers of the developing child. Much of what these people are responsible for is the imposition of socially acceptable behaviour on the individual. In the main parents judge what is right or wrong, good or bad by how they themselves were brought up. Many of these judgments rest of religious beliefs

If we look at psychoanalytical theory the parents or carers are responsible for developing the Ego out of the Id, imposing on the child what is socially acceptable. In Christian countries the values of society reflect the teaching of the Christian faith. So engrained into the culture of the country are these norms of behaviour that few parents would believe that they are bringing their children following the Christian ethic.

As we shall see in the following chapter Freud thought that the religious beliefs of the parents had a major influence on the personality of the child, in particular what they saw as the behaviour they aught .

Failure to live up to the standards that have been set by the superego causes the individual to resort to mental defense mechanisms to alleviate the anxiety and depression that could develop from not living up to this model. It was from this that some early psychoanalysts thought that sticking to a religion caused more harm than good.

The role of parents in the cognitive approach to personality development is not quite so clear. Whilst the processing of information is innate to the human brain how we judge actions must depend on what our parents have shown us to be correct social behaviour. They will also pass on at the same time cultural values and attitudes. In the main we might think that these values and attitudes would be similar for all people in a society. This is in fact not always the case. Some sub cultural groups in society or religious sects may have different values to the majority of society.

Whilst working in a U.K. prison I did a case study on an old prisoner who had had a string of convictions for theft and burglary. In discussing with him his criminal history he told me that the first time he stole was when he was five years of age. He had been sent to the corner shop to get some bread. When he arrived at the shop he found it empty. Looking around and seeing no one he took the bread and ran back home. When he gave the money back to his mother she asked him how he had got the bread. He told her and she gave him a smack on the legs. If this had been me before my parents the slap would have been because I stole the bread. In this prisoners case he was slapped because he had left the shop without taking the money from the till. Such parental influence on what is right and wrong must have influence the moral development of this man.

With Roger's theory the influence of religion passes from the responsibility of the parents to that of the individual. In religious people the ideal self is, most clearly, has a major religious component. Maslow found that some of the people who most frequently self actualized were those with a deep religious faith. Many of those who live to deeply religious life talked about the feeling of wholeness, satisfaction and a great joy gained form beauty and goodness, all characteristics of self actualizes. Thus Icons of a faith can have a great influence on the believer.

With Wilson's concentration on survival and mating, behaviors that are often deemed innate to all living things, the processes by which these are affected by believe become distinctly unclear. None of the current writers on this theory of personality has given much thought to the role religion plays in personality development but I would assume that there must be some role. For example how we behave towards the opposite sex and how we display our own sexuality is often set by the religion we follow. In Islam the exposure of female flesh is not condoned, nor is the wearing of makeup, hence the reason why we see most Islamic countries women are fully covered. The rationale behind this is so that women will not be sexually exploited by men. This may be fine in cultures where the matching of male and female is undertaken by intermediaries, such as parents, but not in countries where finding a mate is left to the individual.

A similar situation occurs when we look at Trait theory. By implication traits are innate and not learnt. Thus the role of the parent or carer is to ensure that these traits are expressed in a socially acceptable way. What is acceptable depends on what they themselves have been taught as acceptable and this, as said earlier, will mainly reflect the religious beliefs of the family.

In some religions and culture this schooling in religious belief is undertaken in a very strict way and is left to the religious leaders to undertake. One sees this in Orthodox Judaism and the Muslim faith where schooling takes place in a highly disciplined and traditional way. Often the completion of this schooling is marked by some rite of passage that moves the person from childhood to adult life. To a lesser extent this is also seen in the Christian faith, with Sunday school and confirmation.

From all the above what becomes clear is that shaping a persons personality starts at some point and is mould either by the parents and what they believe in or by the environment in which the person grows up in or a combination of the two. What also becomes clear is that in this developing process and in adult life there will be, on occasions, frictions between who were perceive we are, how we would like to be and what society expects of us. These frictions often lead on to frustrations and anxieties that will need to be dealt with at some point.

This is in fact termed "Cognitive Dissonance" and is where two cognitions or thoughts that are in opposition to each other, resulting in disharmony in the individual (Festinger 1957) According to

Festinger , the human state is always looking for consistency and stasis. When inconsistency or imbalance occurs then the human state is to try and resolve it. Usually this is by taking the easiest route out of dissonance i.e. a change of attitude or behaviour. Thus socially acceptable behaviour is maintained. In some cases this is not true and the individual demonstrates an unacceptable way of behaving. The result of this is in some individuals is the development of personality disorders such as psychopathic or sociopathic behaviors.

Religious Thought and Feelings

Thoughts are streams of consciousness that we hear in our mind and are f two basic types. Imaginative thought speaks for itself, whilst propositional thought is concerned with claims and propositions. Thinking depends on the development of concepts because thought is not concrete but abstract. Many of these concepts come from our culture included in which are our religious beliefs. In Christians cultures the concept of some form of after live is shaped by believe. Thus if we think about heaven or hell it will, in the main, be a Christian concept of what these will be like. Thus our beliefs shape our imaginative thought but they also affect our propositional thought. In planning actions and intentions and thinking about consequences much of the thinking involved in this process will be shaped by religious or cultural teaching. If we harm someone we know that there will be punishment but it is not the punishment that often stops us from harming it is the moral and emotional effects that our actions have on the individual that shapes the behaviour and this form of thinking will be shaped by belief.

There are many things in life that are beyond understanding of most humans. In the past these would be put down to acts of god, indeed most household insurance policies still talk about acts of God. One of the key things that thought allows us to do is to thing over events that have happened and learn from them. This is in fact a survival mechanism, for if we were unable to learn from our experiences we would not survive. However there are occasions when things happen that are almost without explanation. It is at these times that we need to find some reason for the event happening. Human thinking finds it very difficult to cope without resolution to situations. We often talk these days about "closure". In Northern Ireland in the 1970's people were taken form their homes and were never seen again. The families were left wondering what had happened to them. Time, rather than being the great healer in this situation, made the need to find out what happened more intense. In almost every case when the family were asked why they were still looking they talked about the need for "closure". The need to see a body; to know where the loved one rests. In cases where this is not possible people often find that having a religious belief allows that closure to happen. Phrases such as, "It was God's will" or "whilst I do not know, I know that God does" are common in these situations. Our beliefs allow us to work out logic to events and whilst we might not understand the reason they allow closure to happen, relieving tension, fear and anxiety in the individual. Research has shown that people without a belief in God find closure in these situations more difficult to achieve and therefore suffer greater anxiety

Therefore scripture gives to the faithful a means of explaining almost every thing. If this is the case then it is a two edged sword, for whilst on the one hand will give a good rational explanation to some behaviors both in humans and events in nature how can it explain away the deaths of say, hundreds of children in the disasters, such a s happened in Aberfan, in Wales in the 1960's. Christians believe in a loving God and such events causes a great cognitive dissonance in the individual and communities at large. Without belief this situation becomes almost impossible to understand. However many ministers in that area at the time talked about the event being "man made" and the response being God inspired. The same is also true following the events of 9/11. God works through the evil created by man to good for mankind. It is only through seeing the unexplained in this light that faith allows the believer to continue in the concept of the God they believe in and give "Wholeness" to their faith, behaviour and vision of the world.

References:

Smith.E.(2003) Atkinsons & Hilgard "Introduction to Psychology"Thomson.**Wadworth**. Boston USA page 454.

Allport.G.W. & Odbert.H.S. (1936) Trait Names;A Psychological Study, Psychological Monograms,47 (1,Whole No.211)

Cattell.R.B.(1957) Personality and Motivation Structure Measurement, Yonkers – on – Hudson, NY:World.

Freud.S. (1901) Psychopathology of Everyday Life,(Standard edition vol.6) London: Hogarth press

Carlson.R.(1971) Where is the person in personality research? Psychology Bulletin. 75 pp 203-219

Bandura.A.(1986) Social Foundations of thought and action: A Social Cognitive Theory. Englewood Cliffs;NJ: Prentice-Hall

Wilson.E.O.(1975) Sociobiology: The New Synthesis. Cambridge MA: Harvard University Press.

Buss,D.M. & Barnes,M.(1986) Preferences in Mate Selection, Journal of Personality and Socila Psychology, 50, 559-570

Ozer,D.J. & Reise,S.P. (1994) Personality assessment, Annual review of Psychology, 45, 357 – 388

McCrae.R.R. & Costa,P.T.(1999) a Five factor Theory of personality across instruments and observers, Journal of Personality & Research, New York, Guildford.

Festinger,L.(1957) A Theory of Cognitive Dissonance, Stanford: Stanford University Press.

Eysank,H.J.(1953) The Structure of Personality, New York, Wiley.

Chapter 4:

PERSONALITY THEORISTS AND THE RELIGIOUS EXPERIENCE

Freud 1856-1939

At the time that most of the personality theorist were writing and developing their theories religion, especially the Christian religion were still very dominant in the European culture of their day. Freud was born and brought up in the catholic culture of Vienna, as were many of the patients that he based his observations on. Freud was in fact a Jew, although he had little interest in the faith, he must have been influenced by it.

It was only in the later years that his thoughts turned back to religion and his own faith. Byrnes (1984) tells of the correspondence that Freud had with a young doctor who had a religious experience resulting in his conversion to active Christianity. The young doctor wrote to Freud:

I am writing to tell you of an experience that I had in the year I Graduated at the University of X. One afternoon while I was

passing through the dissecting room my attention was attracted to a sweet – faced dear old lady who was being carried to the dissecting table. This sweet faced woman made such an impression on me that a thought flashed through my mind," there is no God: if there were a God he would not have allowed this dear old woman to be brought into the dissecting room.

When I got home that afternoon the feeling I had had at the sight in the dissecting room had determined me to discontinue going to church. The doctrines of Christianity had before this been the subject of doubts in my mind.

While I was meditating on this matter a voice spoke to my soul that," I should consider the step I was about to take." My spirit replied to this inner voice saying," If I knew of a certainty that Christianity was truth and the Bible was the Word of God, then I would accept it."

In the course of the next few days God made it clear to my soul that the Bible was His Word, that the teaching about Jesus Christ was true, and that Jesus was our only hope. After such a clear revelation I accepted the Bible as God's Word and Jesus as my personal savior. Since then God has revealed himself to me by many infallible proofs.

(Freud 1959b 243 – 44)

Readers Activity

From what you read in the previous chapter what do you think Freud's answer to this letter might have been? Write down a few ideas of what he might have included.

In reply Freud told the young doctor that such behaviour was quite understandable for what the young man experienced as he passed through the dissecting room was a visual expression of the conflicts that were raging within his subconscious. What is needed is some resolution of that conflict and this young man experienced when he accepts Christ as his personal Lord and Savior. For Freud this was what religion offered us, a way of resolving conflicts that occur in our thinking and experience that cannot be resolved by normal thinking or behaviour. If you want, it was another mental defense mechanism.

Freud saw the religious experience as a projection of a father figure who had the ability to shield and defend the individual from conflicts in our personal and social life. This concept of defender was quite common in the mid to late 18th century. The great hymn writer, Robert Grant, in his hymn O worship the King has these words:-

Our shield and defender…
Our Maker, defender, Redeemer & friend

In much of Freud's later writing he talks about the two sides of religion, the formation of beliefs and the development of ethical behaviour. The formation of beliefs were, in the main about mechanisms that would allow conflict resolution whilst ethical behaviour resulted out of beliefs and allowed for conflict to be avoided in the first place. It was as if life and the universe was a screen on which images could be projected, their consequences thought about, and an outcome decided upon.

This idea of God as father is fine if you have a normative concept of a father. But what happens if as a young child you had an abusing father and your image of a father is very negative and threatening? This would make belief in a Father God very difficult to hold. It would cause major conflict within the conscious and subconscious that would make holding a belief quite difficult.

In our review of Freud's work in the last chapter we talked the Oedipus complex. This is when the child loves the mother so much that they see the father as a threat and rival for the attention and love of the mother. The resolution comes later when the child resolves the conflict by seeing the father is a figure to be idolized, "My dad is better than your dad" and so on. Freud pointed out that this, so called Deification of the father figure has been seen throughout history. From this he postulated that for millennia we had lived as tribes under the dominance of a single violent chief. When such a father figure was lost it became necessary to invent one, an idol or god. Freud thought that all of this left what he called Memory Traces in the modern mind. This combined with the father image that we develop from our own experiences then form to give us our own image of God.

In mans development it also became clear that there was also an awesomeness in nature that man had no control over and no defense from. In his book "Future of an Illusion", Freud points out that we soon discover in adult life that we remain children and have no protection against superior powers such as nature. Our defenselessness leads us to create images of gods whom we dread but in whom we trust, as indeed we might see a father.

At times of fear and anxiety it is often found that individuals find comfort from doing things that are familiar and repetitive. Freud thought he saw this in religious practice and tried over many years to link this with obsessive compulsive behaviour. He attempted to call religious observance "Universal Obsess ional Neurosis" For Freud religion was invented as a mechanism that allowed believers to cope in difficult circumstances and situations. It was born out of the reverence and fear of the personal experience of human fathers along with a reverence and fear of the world in which we live. From this comes a cosmic Father figure with appropriate religious practices such as worship and sacrifice so appease the god and keep him happy.

In the later half of the 20th century and the beginning of the 21st there has been a major emasculation of the role of the father in the family. Whilst there are many explanations for this role softening it has given rise to what is called the "New Man". This is, in the main, seen as where a man takes on some of the role of the mother and shares in domestic duties and child rearing. At the same time there has also been an emasculation of the father figure in God. Prayers have been written addressing the Christian deity as "Our Father and Mother in God". In St. Patrick's Cathedral in New York there is a sculpture depicting God as a woman.

It is possible in Freud's writing to see elements of his religious background coming through. For example he talks about repressions and projections when illustrating how the images of gods are formed. As we illustrated early there is also an element of the Oedipus complex coming through in the relationship between gods and humans. In more recent times there has been discussion that the superegos, the highly moral regulator of conduct, and is our internal god created from the rewards and punishments administered to us in our lifetimes. The role then of the ego is to become the ethical and moral arbiter of behaviour shaped by religious belief or the lack of it.

Jung 1875-1961

Jung was a contemporary of Freud and the two corresponded as they developed their not too dissimilar theories. However, whilst the two started out as friends colleagues as life progressed there was a wide divergence of views which left the pair at the end of their lives antagonistic towards each other. Jung was born and brought up in Basel, the son of a clergyman. From a very early age he had been immersed in religious life and thinking. It was no wonder then that he showed a great interest in theology and mysticism during his medical studies.

Jung's ideas about the structure of the psyche and the ways people achieve their potential are very much based on his view of religion. From the psyche comes the archetypes, that give us an mage of God, and thus religious faith. Some of these archetypes are almost universal to a community, for example the image of God as an old man. This Jung called this "the collective psyche"; archetypes that we all recognize. He saw that religions were mainly concerned with devils, saviors and the like and these have reflections in the thinking of each and every one of us.

The image of the church as a building and as a group of people also has a very important function psychologically. So much of what is seen as religious rites of the church are in fact rites of passage in the community. Baptism is not only an entry to the church but also an acceptable of the child into the community. Confirmation or admission to church membership often signifies the move from childhood to adult life. Funerals are the way to the afterlife and allow the living to sever the bonds that have existed with the dead.

Archetypes also exist in the lives of the saints. In an earlier chapter we talked about the need for saints as examples of lives to look up to. Jung sees these as archetypes and extremely important in the development of a religious ethic. They are the yardsticks that allow us to measure how well we are doing in our own religious life. They become heroes and in so doing energize us in our supreme archetype in ourselves, our personality.

Jung thought that the closer we grew to knowing ourselves the closer we came to harmony with ourselves. He saw the Self as an intellectual construct that served to express an unknowable essence that we cannot grasp, since by definition it transcends our powers of comprehension. It might equally be called "God within us" (1972, p238).

Much of Jung's thinking came out of introspection and self

examination of his own thoughts and feeling. There is little doubt that his early years played an important part in shaping that thinking. In more recent years, mainly because much of Jung's writing is complex there has been a radical re examination of his work. In particular there has been a re evaluation of his thinking about God and such archetypes as, "The soul". Byrnes (1984) gives a good summary when he wrote

> ***Authors have examined how Christ is a paradigm for the individual ego (Edinger 1973) and how the religious symbols represent a genuine religious logic (Mosier 1968 – 69). A number of studies of religious symbols within tradition suggest ways of dealing with a God image …***

This type of detailed study of Jung's work has allowed us to apply more closely the writings of this great mind to the religious experience.

Allport 1897-1967

With Freud and Jung we have to eminent people who were closely linked in time and geography and who actually had the opportunity to discuss their thoughts and findings and give insights to each others work. The fact that this drove them to dislike each other is beside the point, but one does get the feeling that each had an influence on the other that enhanced their work and writing.

The same is not true for our next couple. As far as I can discern they never met and did not write to each other and yet they both concerned themselves with the self – transcending possibilities of freely expressed individuality in a given environment. For them it was all about goals and the future. They both chose to describe personality by accenting the goals of the individual.

Gordon Allport was an American from a fairly wealthy family in Indiana. According to Allport the ethic of the family was hard work and steadfast belief in God. He was brought up in a protestant home who believed that all problems could be solved if placed in God's hands and prayed about. The family believed in a "muscular" Christianity which meant that they often helped people who were in trouble. Is it any wonder then that when he went to university at Harvard, he studied psychology and social work? He said himself that he just simply liked helping people. However Allport was not immune form the influences of Freud and Jung because he spent his PhD year studying in Germany.

Allport believed that religion represented the highest form of human striving for a goal. To be religious was the ultimate in the human condition and to have a personality that demonstrated a conscience the ultimate need to attaining that goal. For Allport religion was the driving force to the discovery of goodness and religious practice the mechanism for achieving that goal. Prayer focuses faith, sometimes allowing the person praying to self reflect and at other times to concentrate on inner energies and activities that develop a godly state of the mind. He also saw religion as the great unifying force and also the drive that pushed people and communities often beyond themselves to achieve a greater good than would be possible by oneself.

To have faith, according to Allport is one of the strongest possible mental states to have. Not only does it drive one on but it also made one set goals that were good, self denying and for the greater good of all. He also thought that faith allowed us to cope with emotions more realistically and a fuller meaning to life. In much of his work he saw that faith gave people a healthier outlook on life and seemed to make individuals more polite and less aggressive. He game some examples of religious communities in America where crime and violence were almost non existent.

Allport felt that one could see mature religious sentiment in people by observing various traits. For example altruistic behaviour is a very high order trait in the religious. So is the ability to be uncritical when looking at the workings of the world. Both of these allow the individual to go and work with the socially deprived in conditions that others would find appalling. In so doing Allport comes back to his routes and his love of working for other people. He wrote this:

> ***Faith is basically man's belief in the validity and attainability of some goal! Goals are set by desires; Desires... are not merely pushes from behind but include such complex future oriented states as longing for a better world, for ones own perfection, for a completely satisfying relation to the universe (1950 pp149)***

Of equal interest is how Allport viewed the image of God. He had very little time for the idea of a father figure or old man and I guess if he was around today he would have little truck wit the idea of God being female. For him God was not about human form or function but more about the concept of a driving force of personality that might rule over the whole universe. This closely matched his own image of the human existence. The body was the temple of the soul, but what was the soul? Allport believed that the soul of an individual was their personality. For him personality was the driving force that shaped the individual to being a unique being. If we remember people we not only remember how they looked but also what they did and how they did it. These later points were the ones that made us who we are. We might have doppelgangers in abundance but none would be exactly the same as us. It is often what we do that long outlives our life. Allports thinking at this point reminds me of the quote, "By their deed shall ye know them". People are often remembered for what they did and not what they looked like. Who would recognize a picture of Freud and yet he is universally know for his work.

Perhaps the area that illustrates best the integration of Allports theory of personality and his religious belief was when he talked about the development of the "Conscience". Unlike Freud who says this as just a mechanism for developing obedience, Allport saw the conscience as a much higher order of behaviour. In fact for him it was the goal or religious behaviour. Conscience develops as the individual matures and out of its influence comes moral behaviour. For Allport key to this process is the setting of long term goals and an ideal self image. Allport called this collective a "values schema"

In developing the conscience important changes occur, sanctions move from the external to the internal; experience moves from what has happened to what could and what should; and behaviour moves from self gratification to altruism. An overall integrity and an ongoing search to discover the unity of being become the goal of such individuals. From this Allport concluded that the knowledge of what is right and wrong is not innate but has to be learnt and that learning determines how well our conscience develops.

Readers Activity

Look again at Maslows "Hierarchy of Needs and see if you can think of how the religious experience might fit into the levels of his hierarchy. You might also like to draw up a short hierarchy of what you think are religious needs.

Maslow 1908-1970

Abraham Maslow's upbringing was in total contrast to that of Allport. Maslow was the son of a Jewish immigrant family and lived in a non Jewish community in Brooklyn, New York. He went to study psychology at the University of Wisconsin and was very much under the influence of such famous names as Watson, Thorndyke and Hull all of whom were eminent in the behaviorist school of psychology. Maslow considered that behaviorism and psychoanalytical theory were too rigid in their application of theory and seemed mainly concerned with illness. He wanted to prove that human beings were capable of something grander than war and prejudice. He said,

> ***I want to make science consider all the problems that non-scientist have to handle – religion, poetry, values, philosophy and art. 1968 pp55***

He wanted to improve the quality of human existence and this could only be achieved by improving our knowledge about the human condition. Thus, for most of his life he took aspects of human existence, including religion and tried to theorize about them. He, like Allport, thought that religion was the peak of human experience. As was pointed out in the last chapter he called these fleeting moments of ultimate experience, Self Actualization. They could be caused by seeing a wonderful sunset through to having a mystical vision or experience. Often at these moments the individual gained deep insights into the human condition, which radically changed how they lived and perceived the world.

Maslow concerned himself with two levels of human functioning. He talked about, "survival tendencies" and "actualization tendencies". The survival tendency is that which drives us towards satisfaction and the need to ensure that we physically and psychologically survive. Fundamental to survival were needs that had to be fulfilled, such as food, warmth, water; safety needs and the avoidance of pain. The need to feel a sense of belonging and love and intimacy were also extremely important. Only when these were fulfilled could one move on and develop through the hierarchy.

The Actualization tendency develops from the survival tendency.

This drives the individual to develop special capabilities of a higher order. Maslow called this "growth motivation" as the individual does much more than just "get by". According to Maslow Self Actualization follows a genetic blueprint which includes the ability to appreciate beauty, art and good behaviour as part of the religious belief and behaviour.

In his later life he widened this thinking into attempting to give meaning to life. He thought that these peak experiences were what life was all about. He said that these times had a special flavor that we strove to create again and again. One way to do this is through religious ceremony where, through music, drama and vision, peak experiences can be recreated. At these points some people feel so moved that they feel closer to God.

Religion also gave to life a system of values and these, Maslow believed, were basic to human nature.

Thus, when looking at Maslow's hierarchy of human needs we need to look at it not only as a hierarchy but also a measure of human psychological growth. The Self Actualized religious person possesses and develops a variety of good qualities. They will accept themselves for who they are as indeed they do others and the world around them. Their goal in life, as said earlier, is to make things better. They do this not just by prayer and meditation but also by actually getting down to altruistic tasks, raising money, volunteering and the like. They also have the ability to empathize with others and in so doing realize the plight that others find themselves in and do something about it.

The religious also self actualize in other ways. Many are highly creative and, thus, express their faith in music, poetry and the visual and dramatic arts. In the 18th century, when women were not allowed to play a full role in religious life, they often devoted themselves to hymn writing. Nearly all the top ten hymns in a BBC poll in 2001 were written by women at about this time. Where would the festival of nine lessons and carols from Kings College, Cambridge, be without, "O Little Town Of Bethlehem" by Mrs. Alexander or Good Friday without, "There is a Green Hill". It was one of the few ways that they could achieve Self Actualization

What is so rewarding about Maslow's work is that it gives such a positive feel to human nature so much so that some have accused Maslow of looking through rose tinted spectacle. Yet it is difficult to refute that there is a hierarchy to our needs. Human experience has shown that in times of war and famine we revert to our basic needs and instincts and in times of wealth and plenty we achieve some of our greatest work.

Eysenck 1916-1997

Hans Eysenck was born in Germany in 1916. His parents were actors who divorced when he was only two and Hans was raised by his grandmother. He left Germany when he was 18 when the Nazis came to power because, as an active Jewish sympathizer his life was at risk. He cam to England and studied throughout the war at London University and received his PhD in Psychology in 1940. Throughout his professional life he was antagonistic towards main-stream clinical psychology. He became director of the psychology department at The Institute of Psychiatry at the Bethlehem Royal Hospital, London.

Although a prolific writer it has been very difficult to find anything that he has written specifically about religion in relation to his theory. However through his writings we do get little glimpses of his thinking. Raj Persaud broadcaster and consultant psychiatrist at the Maudsley Hospital, writing in the Daily Telegraph on March 24th 2003 talks about some of Eysenck's early work. He undertook a study of clinical therapy at the Maudsley Hospital comparing the improvement rates of thousands of people undergoing psychotherapy with a control group who had similar psychological problems, but who merely remained on the waiting list.

Whilst 64% of the patients receiving therapy improved so did 72% of those who were in the control group with no therapy at all. Eysenck, like Persuad, put the growth of therapy over the later half of the 20th century down to the breakdown in relationships and the decline of religion. From this and the knowledge that Eysenck was an active Jewish sympathizer, we can conclude that he had some interest in religion.

Eysenck was primarily a research psychologist and believed that much of what he saw in peoples personalities was down to genetics and physiologically supported. He therefore went to physiological research to find possible explanations for the differences in personality. Dying as he did in 1997 he was too late to see some of the mysteries of the brain that magnetic imaging was beginning to uncover. I am sure that he would have reveled in the debate that Newburg and others have been developing over the past few years about the brain, behaviour and religion.

The dimensions that he developed based on research and mathematical models left nothing to semantic theory. Indeed he fiercely rebutted anything to do with fantasy, or what he thought was fanatic. For example there appears in the cannon of his work a number of articles and references rebutting Astrology. He did not believe that our personalities could be shaped by the star sign we were born under and the time of the day. He even did some research to see if this was the case but no significant correlations were found.

So what can we draw from his work in relation to the religious experience. In Eysenck's research he found that highly neurotic people were very much focused individuals. They tended to over respond to situations that caused panic and were always looking for way in which to a) reduce the fear and b) resolve the panic that they might suffer. They were also very ritualistic in their behaviour and found comfort from the familiar. If we add to this the introvert – extravert paradigm other personality traits get added. An introverted neurotic would also find great solus from being alone and having long periods of quietness. The stable introvert would enjoy solitude and thinking but would also enjoy writing and sharing their research wit the wider world

The extraverted neurotic would be good at ignoring and forgetting the things that overwhelm them. They would engage in classical defense mechanisms such as denial and repression. They would enjoy stimulation of all the senses, through music, art and literature. The stable extrovert would enjoy all of this but would also like to be the focus of attention and enjoy sharing this experience with others.

Eysenck realized that, although he had used large numbers in his study he had missed out some populations, such as those living in psychiatric hospitals. He began to take his studies into large institutions and in so doing found another factor that needed to be considered which he labeled "psychotism". Like the neuroticism this does not mean one is psychotic only that one has some psychotic traits that made you susceptible given certain circumstances. Within such people Eysenck described recklessness, a disregard for common sense and a high level of inappropriate emotional expression. He also found that there was a degree of obsessive behaviour that bordered at times on fanaticism.

Readers Activity

I am sure that as you have been reading the last few paragraphs you might have had a few ideas of religious experiences and how they might fit with the traits described. Take a few minutes out and see if you can match religious experiences to the personality traits described.

In Eysenck's personality test he displays the traits of personality in a square

Neurotic

Introvert **Extrovert**

Stable

The quarters divide the traits into paradigms or dimensions of personality. Over several years I have given this diagram to students and asked them to mark in each quadrant the types of religious practice that could go with each color. They following are a summary of the results:

Yellow:
Exclusive sects / denominations
Radical / extremist
Fundamentalists

Turquoise:
Main stream denominations / religions
New age religions / non conformists
Communities with social outreach

Purple:
Contemplative Communities
Monks / nuns
Quakers

Orange:
Doomsday cults

You will see from this list that these paradigms of personality do help us to understand how people can be attracted to types of religious practice. It is almost at Jesus said to his disciples, "There are many Mansions in My House"; for every personality type there is a religious practice to suit them within the main faiths and without. Whilst Eysenck did not set out to explain religious observance his description of traits and their arrangement does allow us to see how personality fits into religious practice.

References:

Byrnes,J.F. (1984) The Psychology of Religion, Free Press, New York

Freud,S.(1959b)(1928)"A Religious experience." In collected papers vol.5. Edited by James Strachey, New York, Basic Books

Jung,C.G (1972)(1935, 1943) Two essays on analytic psychology. Translated by R. F. C. Hull, second edition, Princeton. N.J. Princeton University Press.

Allport.G(1950) The Individual and His religion: A Psychological Interpretation. New York, Macmillan

Maslow.A(1968) "A Conversation with Abraham Maslow" Psychology Today, February,pp38ff

Persaud,R.(2003) Growth of therapy tells us something about the breakdown of relationships and the decline of religion and the nuclear family, The Daily Telegraph, 24th March.

Chapter 5:

PSYCHOLOGICAL DEVELOPMENT AND THE INFLUENCE OF RELIGION

Cognitive Development

At the beginning of this book we defined Cognition as the mental act of processing knowledge through the senses and learning from it. Cognitive development is the study of how this ability is acquired and developed in the child and what part the environment plays in that process. Much of this area of psychology has been dominated by the Swiss psychologist Jean Piaget (1896 – 1980). However, before his work was recognized psychologist had no clear idea about how the process of cognition developed. Some believed that is was simply a case of biological maturation whilst others thought it was a nurturing process where the parent taught the child through an interactive process. In both cases the child was seen as a passive participant in the process and had only to wait for the right session to come along to learn what was needed to understand the world.

Piaget's contribution was to acknowledge that the child was not a passive participant but an active and driving force in the process. Much of the observations that he developed came from the study of his own children and, later, his work with children in his studies at university. The other contribution that he made was to demonstrate that there was a staging process that the child had to go through which refined the cognitive processes until they were fully developed at maturity. Piaget described children as "enquiring little scientists" who experimented with the environment in which there lived and had the ability to draw conclusions from their experiments.

From these experiments children develop schemas or theories about the environment around them. When they came across a new situation or object in their environment they have to assimilate this into their current schema. Once done an accommodation is made in that schema that the child has developed. For example, most children are brought up in environments where there are cats and or dogs. Thus the child learns that an animal with four legs, a head and a tail is a dog or cat. At home the child will add to this schema that dogs bark and cats meow. Thus when a child goes out into the countryside and sees in a field a head, four legs and a tail, the initial response is to call out, cat or dog. The person with the child corrects the child and gives the word "sheep" to the animal. The child assimilates the head, four legs and tail with additions information of a bleat and white woolly coat. This may take several interactions to get right but the child eventually makes the accommodation between the information and a new point is added to the schema. The problem then comes that anything in a field is a sheep and it is through further refinements of the schema that the cognitive process is completed (Piaget & Inhelder 1948/1956).

Piaget's Stage Theory

Piaget divided cognitive development into four key stages each of which had sub stages. He called these stages in ascending order, sensorimotor stage, the preoperational stage, the concrete operational stage and the formal operational stage. So let's take a closer look at these stages in a little more detail.

The Sensorimotor Stage (0 – 2 years)

Piaget designated this to last for about the first two years of life and was when the child discovers the relationship between their actions and the effects they have. This starts at day one of life when the child learns that they have the ability to make sound and that when a sound is made something happens. For example, a child cries and may be picked up, cuddled or fed, both of which are pleasant activity. The child also starts to build up a cognitive map of themselves but exploring their body and the close environment around them. In so doing they discover the interface between themselves and the outside world; where the finish and the outside world begins. This learning of cause and effect continues through such activities as playing with dishes at table and throwing things away from themselves.

In the early stages of cognitive development it is believed that the child perceives the world as a series of fleeting images. Once a scene is out of sight it, to the child does not exist. The child has to learn that even out of sight objects continue to exist. Piaget called this the concept of "Object Permanence'. If a favorite toy is placed in front of a child the child, at about 8 months old, will reach for it. If the toy is covered with a cloth the child immediately looses interest in it. The child seems to show no emotion that the toy is gone.

If we move on a few months in the life of the child and repeat the experiment the child will have learnt that the object continues to exist even thought it is covered up. The child will remove the cloth and often smiles at the toy and at the tester. A few months further on to 18 months and if a toy is removed from the child's immediate area the child will conduct a hunt of the area until found. In both these cases the child has developed the concept of Object Permanence

The Preoperational Stage (2 – 7 years)

At the interface between the sensorimotor and preoperational stages the child has been developing the cognitive skills to understand the environment and their role in it. At this time the child will also be using symbols in the form of words and pictures to represent the world around them. As the names suggests the child has not fully learnt the rules or operations that operate in the world in which the child lives. However the child has to develop schemas that allow them to understand what they are seeing and thinking.

A classic example of this is the concept of conservation. This is where the child develops the idea that materials remain the same weight or volume despite the changes that may be made in shape, container or spacing. At about the age of 4 years children have not developed this concept. Piaget believes that preoperational thinking was dominated by visual impressions. To demonstrate this he used three experiments with water, clay and buttons.

In the first two glasses of equal dimensions are filled with the same amount of water. The child is asked if the two glasses have the same amount of water in them. Following this one of the glasses of water is poured into a narrower taller glass. The child is then asked which has more in. At this point the child will say that the narrower, taller glass has more water in. The water is then pores back into the original glass and the amounts compared and the child will say they are the same. Over the years that I have performed this experiment with children it never fails to amaze me at the surprise that dawns on their face at this point.

The Second Experiment is with a ball of clay. The child is given two equal sized balls of clay and asked if they are the same size. After agreement is reached, one of the balls is rolled out into a long snake like appearance. The child is asked then which has more clay in it. At this point the child will point to the large ball as having more it. Once rolled back into a ball the child says they are the same again. The final experiment is with counters or buttons of equal size. These are laid out in two straight rows and the child counts the number of buttons in each row. On agreeing that there are the same number one of the rows has more space added between each button. The child is then asked which has more buttons in it. The child will point to what appears visually to be the longer row. Once the spacing is reduced the child will say that they have the same amount in each row.

Whilst studying children in this age range Piaget observed that children seemed to be unaware of the views of others with whom they operated with. Their needs and wishes are the most important and others needs are subsidiary. Piaget called this "egocentrism". To demonstrate this he developed the "three mountain test" where three mountains of differing height are arranged on a table. In this test the child stands on one side of the table while a doll is placed on the table at various locations. The child is asked to choose from a set of photographs what the view would look like from where the doll is. Before the age of 7 the child chooses a picture similar to the view that he or she is seeing.

Concrete Operational Stage (7 – 12 years)

This stage is mainly characterized by the child achievement of the concepts of conservation and the ability to classify objects according to set criteria. One often sees children at this early ages in this stage sorting toys according to color, size etc. Children also have the ability to think in abstracts. One of the tests that I have used to demonstrate this is to ask children to describe the journey from their house to that of a close friend. One often finds that the description is basic, often lacking fine detail such as house colors, name of pubs etc, but the basics are usually correct. As the child progresses through this stage the ability to draw picture of objects from memory and even to tell fictional stories develop. The word of concrete really does describe what happens at this point. They are only able to describe things that they have actually seen or experience.

The Formal Operational stage (12 years and above)

This stage is from 12 years onwards and is aptly named "formal" as the maturing child embarks with the cognitive processes developed into the adult world. The key points at this stage is that the child is able to use abstract representations and problem solve. What is characteristic of children at this stage is that, when problem solving, they tend to adopt a systematic approach to the problem whilst children still in the Concrete operational stage would adopt a random approach to solving the problem, assuming that they could conceptualize it in the first place. Having this ability also allows the child to develop the ability to make moral judgments.

What the Critics Say about Piaget's Work

Whilst at the time Paiget's stage theory of cognitive development was seen as a major breakthrough in more recent times the tests and assumptions made by him have been challenged. In the main these challenges appear to demonstrate that Piaget underestimated the ability of children. Many of the tasks that he tested require more sophisticated skills than originally thought. For example in the sensorimotor stage memory and visual acuity are required so as to perform the task. Also how do we know what the child is thinking? How do we know that it thinks an object is not there?

There has also been some criticism of the words used in the experiments with children. For example in the conservation tests what does the child understand by the word "more"? Some tests, where the words have been changed such as "greater" for "more", have demonstrated that the children get the answer right. Other factors have demonstrated that Piaget's stages can be achieved at a faster or slower rate. Key to this rate of change has been the age that the child starts school. Despite all of this the main problem has been that the alternative approaches to the study of cognitive development have been inconsistent and there has been no real consensus in the challengers to Paiget's dominance

Alternatives to Piaget's Theory

The opposition to Piaget has taken several routes but all state that his tests failed in so much as they were not testing one factor of cognition but many. Thus the various routes taken have tried to separate out these tasks and develop tests for them.

Knowledge Acquisition Approaches

The developmental psychologists who hold this view believe that children and adults essentially have the same cognitive abilities but what separates them is the level and extent of that knowledge. Chi (1978) demonstrated with chess players from college and 10 year olds that the ability to remember moves and patterns of play was similar between the two groups whilst the ability to remember random number groups was more pronounced in the 18 year old group. He came to the conclusion that the difference between these two groups was not stages of cognitive development but domain specific knowledge. By this he meant that the children were expert in playing chess and thus had a deeper grasp of understanding the organization and construct of the game. This group of developmental psychologists believe that it is increased knowledge of the world that leads to increased ability not the other way around.

The Information Processing Approach

These challengers to Piaget argue that cognitive skills rely on the development of Information Processing Skills. By this they mean the specific ability to gather and analyze information from the environment. From this point on the theory disintegrates as there is no consensus amongst its advocates (Mandler 1983). With no real consensus it is difficult to further explain this approach cogently

Sociocultural Approaches

When first looking at Piaget's definition of cognitive development the role of the environment was mentioned. However, what Piaget meant by this was the immediate environment in which the child operated it did not include the social and cultural environment in which the child is brought up. Yet much of what the child learns and the way in which it is learnt is influence by the social setting and culture of the child. You will remember that Piaget described children as "Inquisitive little scientists". Rogoff (2000) thought that rather than viewing them in this way one should think of them as "A newcomer to a culture who seeks to become a native by learning how to look at social reality through the lens of culture". This then widens the possibilities of what influences our thought processes amongst which must be the influence of religion

Theory of the Mind

As part of development of cognitive processes is the ability to think about what other might be thinking. It is amazing when analyzing behaviour and thought much this activity does occupy our mind. Just think about some of our daily activities, how we dress, look and how we behave, all of these are affected by how we think others perceive us. We also, sometimes criticize how we ourselves are thinking, .i.e. how we have believes in something only to find that that belief was mistaken. This process of thinking about thinking is referred to as "metacognition" or "theory of mind". Psychologists have been intrigued as to how this might develop and a whole raft of experiments have been developed (Flavell 1999). These experiments have aimed to study children's knowledge about emotions, beliefs and intentions and have demonstrated that in early childhood the ability to think about what others might think is very limited but once a child starts to interact with others on a large scale, such as going to school or nursery the ability rapidly develops

Bartsch (1995) believes that, as in Piaget's cognitive development there are stages to the development of metacognition. The first stage is when the child realizes that it has desires and emotions and that these need fulfilling. They also understand that others have feeling and thoughts that they can influence possibly to their advantage but they do not understand how others might be thinking about them. Hence the thinking and behaviour that is most commonly called "The Terrible Two's"

The second stage is about the age of 3 years when children start to talk about beliefs and thoughts as well as their own desires and they also have the ability to decide if things are true or false. Finally at the age of 4 years children begin to understand how others might see them and their behaviour and that people can believe things that do not exist in reality. Wellman (1994) has taken this research a little further and has looked which might happen if a child does not develop a "theory of mind". His key finding was that without this theory of mind the child's ability to understand others feeling and beliefs is absent. The descriptive resulting behaviour resembled those who suffer from Autism, i.e. where children are unresponsive to and communicating with others.

Development of Moral Judgment

Also developing out of Piaget's work was his interest in how children develop their understanding of the moral and social conventions that operate in a given culture. He believes that this development went parallel with their cognitive development. One of the ways that he studied this was by observing children at play

(Piaget 1932/1965). In the first stage he noted that when children participated in "Parallel Play". At this stage each child follows their own private set of rules for play and whilst in the same room with other children do not co operate or participated in other children's play. There is no co operation or competition

By the second stage at the age of about 5 years rules become important to a child's play. These rules tend to be absolute and unchangeable and give to the child a set of certainties by which to judge the action of others. At this stage the child sees actions and results as the deciding factor and not the intention. Piaget gave children at this stage a set of stories that had both result and intent, i.e. stealing food to feed a hungry person and breaking cups in the process. In every case it was the braking of cups that was the deciding factor regardless of why the food was stolen.

By the third stage from the age of 8 years onwards all the rules and conventions have been learnt and the child has the ability to appreciate the rules and conventions of society and use them in co operating with others. When making judgments they also have the ability to look at intentions as well as outcomes. By the formal operational stage of development not only dues the child understand rules and conventions but also has the ability to generate new rules and conventions to meet the needs of their particular circumstance at that time. However, Piaget says that at this stage children tend to be somewhat idealistic and it is only with maturity that this changes.

The work of Lawrence Kohlberg

For Piaget his work on moral development was really a side issue to that of his main work. It was left to Kohlberg, an American, to develop the work further and look at moral reasoning amongst adolescents and young adults. Like Piaget he looked for universal stages in the development of moral judgments. Much of his testing was similar to Piaget whereby he set stories that had both intent and result that created dilemmas for the participants. By analyzing the answers Kohlberg (1967/11976) arrived at six stages of moral development which he grouped into three levels, the **Preconventional, Conventional** and **Postconventional**

Kohlberg reported that only about 10% of adults actually reached stage6 and showed clear principled thinking. Kohlberg also conducted his research across cultures and the sexual divide. However this has not stopped other criticizing his work on the basis of culture and male dominance in its language. Kohlberg's work does, however, act as a useful adjunct to that of Piaget.

Erikson: Emotional & Motivational Development

Erik Erikson will best be remembered as the psychologist who placed the term "Identity Crisis the psychology vocabulary. His work looked at the emotional and motivational development of children. Key to his work was the belief that everything that lived has ground plan and that everything has a time for acquisition and ascendancy. At the beginning we have all the emotions and motivations that are required in their basic form. As we grow and develop elements become operational at different points in our lives and may take centre stage. What development does is allow us to learn how to use and exploit these elements to our own best advantage.

Whilst Piaget looked at cognitive development Erickson concentrated of socio emotional development and as a consequence looked more closely at the personality rather than the mental functioning of children. He saw various stages to the emotional development in which conflicting emotions could be taking centre stage.

These were

Infancy (0-1 ½) Basic trust vs. Basic mistrust (hope)
Early Childhood (2 – 6) Autonomy vs. shame and doubt (will)
Initiative vs. guilt (purpose)
Childhood (7 – 12) Industry vs. Inferiority (Competence)
Adolescence (13 – 21) Identity vs. role confusion (fidelity)
Young Adult (21 – 35) Intimacy vs. isolation (love)
Adulthood (35 – 60) General activity vs. stagnation (care)
Maturity (60 +) Integrity vs. despair (Wisdom)

These conflicts then generate within us motivational forces (in brackets) that drive us forward.(Erikson 1963)

If we take a look at just one of these stages it is possible to get a flavor of Erikson's hypothesis. He believed that the major task confronting adolescents was the question, "Who am I" and "Where is my life going". This is a major crunch time in our lives and arises out of the conflict between discovering our identity and the role confusion when neither a child nor an adult. Thus one of the things that we look for at this time is fidelity in our relationships. Similarly at the maturity stage one often finds older people concerned about the state of the world and modern living. They feel that they should fight for standards and a preservation of their integrity and this motivates them to dispense wisdom to the generations that come after them.

This staged approach has been described by some as similar to Shakespeare's seven ages of man. In reading much of what Erikson has written there is a feeling that much of what he has written has a religious flavor to it, as indeed does some of the work done by Piaget, in particular his concept of moral judgment.

Erikson thought that the idea of trust and mistrust came from the way that babies are handled in the early years of life. As the child is fed and cuddled it builds up trust between the prime carer and itself.

When not fed our neglected the child learns the concept of mistrust. However the child always lives in hope of being cared for. As life moves on and the child establishes a wider radius of experiences they develop language that allows them to question and discover roles and relationships. This expands they imagination and allows them to think about roles for themselves. They thus emerge with a sense of initiative as a basis for a realistic sense of ambition and purpose.

Gender Identity, Personality and Religious Development

Part of this role identity has to be the beliefs that the role model has. In the early stages of our emotional development that models are often our parents. However, as we develop and expand our relationships our role models change. For example in our teenage years, at the time Erikson says we are looking for fidelity in our relationships a role model with strong religious beliefs will have a greater influence that our parents. Such loyalty and friendship enables the adolescent to preserve their orientation to the divine image and their need for support.

Another key aspect in our emotional development is their identify of our gender and the role that gender allows up to play. Erikson talks about the concept of "genital maturity". Before genital maturity, much of our sex life is of the self seeking, identity – hungry type, with each partner trying to reach satisfaction. In so doing the act is combative and often ends in triumph or defeat. With the genital mature the act is more loving, caring and shared activity often with the partners giving to each other and having little concern for their own satisfaction.

At each stage of our emotional development the influence of religion has some effect. How we are cared for, what values shape our parents behaviour all have an impact on how we see ourselves, our sexuality and our sexual behaviour. Most faiths have some taboo over same sex relationships and the perversion of the sexual act. Thus if we are exposed to the such teachings they will have an effect on how we see our sexuality and our sexual behaviour. In England, when Christian principles were very dominant to declare that one was homosexual was a sure recipe for personal and social disaster. Today such sexual behaviour is seen by many as not being a problem. Indeed the government have attempted to legislate that such relationships have the same rights as heterosexual couples.

Erikson believes that same sex attraction and sexual deviation arise out of unsuccessful or abnormal events at the stages of emotional development. Thus the expression of sexuality and sexual function is a result of the interplay between self expression, satisfaction and religious belief. The type of trust developed in early life leads to a proper balance between identity and intimacy, both of which very much determine how the individual sees themselves in relationship to God. Erikson also believed that the identity and intimacy determine how people form the religious belief and behaviour of the next generation.

The Work of Fowler and the Development of Faith

One can see from what has been written above that the work of Piaget, Kohlberg and Erikson has some bearing on the development of faith and religious belief. The problem is that one has to extrapolate this from the findings rather than the meaning being explicit. Inspire by the reading of the works of these three psychologist, James Fowler took their theories and from them and his experience as a Christian minister developed a stage theory of the development of faith which he published in a book entitled, Stages of Faith (1981).

Fowler saw that faith went through a number of defined stages from the time we are born to the time we die. These stage can be aligned to those of Piaget, Erikson and Kohlberg and when reading Fowler's description it is a good idea to read them with the other theories in mind.

Pre Stage ***Undifferentiated Faith*** *(birth to 1 ½ years)*

For the first year or so of life there is only one God figure in the life of a child and that is the prime carer. All the needs and wants of the child are met by this one figure. There is a mutuality in the relationship where one gives and the other receives. The child learns that there are greater powers in the world and that we owe gratitude and thanks to those greater powers. The child also learns that they are part of a greater family and part of that family existence is that one has to trust and have faith in the other members. To the child the prime carers are all powerful and all giving but also have the ability to reward good and punish bad.

Stage 1 ***Introjective – Projective Faith*** *(2 – 6 years)*

At about this age, as we have already seen, language development allows the child to express emotions and feelings. Often one finds that the child creates around them a fantasy filled world full of uninhibited thoughts and feelings devoid of any logic. The child's awareness is quite centered on themselves. Children at this stage love fairy tales and equate Bible stories on a similar level. Whilst, particularly with boys, the stories are rather gruesome, and contain death and scary incidents they see themselves as immortal and will live for ever, despite the fact that they might have encountered death through relatives and family pets.

Stage 2 ***Mythic – Literal Faith*** *(7 – 12 years)*

Fowler describes in his book how he found at this point, when talking to children about their view of God a marked similarity to the role of the head of a family. All the stories that the child has heard about in relation to faith are taken at a literal level and their interpretation and imagery is related to the family and culture that the child has been brought up in. In so doing the child is seeking a consistency between what they experience here on earth and what might be happening in heaven. In his studies of children Fowler found that they had great difficulty in separating out the role of the head of the household and that of God. It seemed that God has a few greater roles such as making day and night happen and the seasons to develop but other than that he is just like dad or mom. At the transition from this to stage three children also realize that they are not immortal and will die. This often causes great fear and fretting in the child often expressed as night terrors or bad dreams

Stage 3 ***Synthetic – Conventional Faith*** *(13 – 21 years)*

By the teenage years the young adult is being exposed to a greater number of outside forces in their environment. Gone is the supremacy of the family and family values and these are now judged alongside those set by the school, pear group, and organizations that the young adult participates in. Thus there is a great questioning of faith and belief. This may also be a time of experimentation of other beliefs and denominations. From this will come positive and negative effects, their faith may be enhanced or changed to disbelief.

Stage 4 ***Individuative – Reflective Faith*** *(21 – 35 years)*

By this time role identity and individuality have been established with the individual making a distinct contribution to the world. They may also have children and be a god figure to others. It is found that adults at this time look for similar groups that have the same values as themselves and want a supportative environment in which to express their faith and to bring their family up in. There is a deepening of faith at this point and a greater quest to understand the meaning of faith to them and their life.

Stage 5 ***Conjunctive Faith*** *(35 – 60 years)*

Not all adults reach these last two stages fully. By this time the adult has achieved and faced challenges and overcome hardships and have been subject to the will of other adults. They will have developed a high moral sense which will have been shaped by their faith and belief. Fowler saw this stage as putting faith into action by good works or through bringing others into the faith. In religious terms this often is the highly productive time in faith mainly because believers have time, money and energy to devote to their faith and belief.

Stage 6 ***Universalizing Faith*** *(60+)*

This is a time of anticipation and reflection on life; anticipation on what is to come after death and reflection on a life lived. It may be a time for making amends and pardoning wrongs as well as a time of living a faith in its fullest meaning.

Fowler saw these stages similar to the hierarchy of needs we looked at in a previous chapter. For him they were stages to an ultimate goal; the prize that our faith offers. As an attempt to describe how faith develops they have some worth but hey also have some dangers. For exampled, by putting stages to ages is he putting faith development into a straight jacket? Others have found that, depending on the rigors of an individuals life will depend on when they question fait hand the existence of a god. Never the less this attempt to chart the development of faith can be quite useful to those working with young people.

References:

Piaget.J & Inhelder.B. (1948) The child's concept of space, London, Routlege & Keagan

Paul Piaget.J (1932/1965) The Moral Jidgement of the child, New York, Free Press

Chi.M.(1978) Knowledge structures and memory development. In R.S. Siegler (ed) Children's thinking, what develops. Hillsdale, NJ: Erlbaum

Mandler.J(1983) Representation. In P.H. Mussen (ed) Handbook on Child Psychology (vol. 3) New York: Wiley

Rogoff.B(2000) Culture and development. New York. Oxford University Press

Flavell.J.H.(1999) Cognitive Development: Children's Knowledge About the mind,
Annual review of Psychology, 50, 21 -45

Kohlberg.L.(1969 1976) Moral Stages & Moralisation: The Cognitive development Approach. In T. Lickong (ed) Moral Development and Behaviour. New York: Holt, Rinehart & Winston.

Erikson.E.(1963) Childhood and Society (2nd Ed) Cambridge, MA, MIT Press

Erikson.E.(1968) Identity: Youth and Crisis. New York. Norton.

Fowler.J (1981)Stages of Faith; the psychology of human development and the quest for meaning. New York: Harper Row

Bartsch.K. & Wellman.H.M. (1995) Children talk about the mind. New York. Oxford University Press

Wellman. H.M.(1994) Early Understanding of the mind: The normal case. In S. Baron-Cohen (ed) Understanding other minds: Perspectives from Autism. (pp10–39) New York Oxford University press

Chapter 6

SOCIAL DEVELOPMENT AND THE INFLUENCE OF RELIGION

Early Social Development

The social environments in which we develop and operate have a huge impact on us and how we behave. Every time we go to church or attend an activity we not only commune with the people we meet, but we also further refine and update of behaviour within that group. This process starts from the very beginning of our life on the day we are born and does not stop until the day we die. With such an importance it is no wonder that psychologists have paid such attention to such issues as attachment, parenting styles and social interaction. These subjects are intrinsically linked but to understand them we need to look at the separately.

Attachment Theory

The term attachment is used to describe the behaviour demonstrated between carer and baby so as to seek closeness and security with its carers. Usually this is with the mother as the prime carer and develops mainly out of the provision of food, warmth and a feeling of security, or so we thought! Experiments have demonstrated that attachment does not come from the provision of food alone. For example, some animals feed themselves from birth, but still have a need for parents.

Harlow (1969) conducted an experiment where infant monkeys were separated from their mothers at birth placed on two artificial mothers made out of wire. One was covered with soft toweling and the other provided food, but was bare wire. Both looked monkey like and had wooden heads. The experiment was to determine whether the young monkeys would cling to the "mother" that was the feeder or the toweling mother. Much to the surprise of the experimenters the monkey did not attach to the feeding "mother" but the soft toweling "mother". This passive non feeding "mother" provided for the infant monkey a source of security. The experiment was taken further to see how long the monkeys would use the passive toweling "mother". The experiment found that the attachment lasted almost as long as that of attachment within the normal monkey population. However, it was later noted that the monkeys artificially reared had problems in other aspects of their social behaviour. They had great problems with social interactions and the ability to bond with other monkeys. They were also found to be very aggressive and have poor social skills. Female monkeys had difficulty in rearing children and often abandoned their new born babies.

Some have taken these findings and applied them to the abnormal behaviour seen with children who have been raised in a social setting where parenting contact is greatly reduced, i.e. in children's homes or working families. To do so is too simplistic an approach but, as we shall see later, there are some elements that these children and the monkeys have in common. Much of the work in this area was done in the 1950's by John Bowlby. He became interested in attachment when watching babies and children in hospital wards and nurseries, particularly when they were separated from their mothers, for example when in long term neonatal care. His findings demonstrated that good attachments were essential to the well being and development of good social relations for adult life. (Bowlby 1975)

Bowlby's work was further developed by one of his assistants, Mary Ainsworth (1978), who studied mother and child attachment in Uganda and the USA. From this she was able to develop a series of laboratory experiments based on placing the child in strange situations, hence the name of the experiments "the strange situation" tests. From this she was able develop categories of attachment. The categories were as follows:

Securely Attached:- When the child shows distress at the mother leaving and seeking interaction when she returns. These may be physical or social.

Insecurely Attached, Avoidant:- These children avoid interacting with the mother during reunion. Some ignore the mother altogether, others display mixed interactions.

Insecurely Attached, Ambivalent:- These children show resistance to the mother during reunion episodes. They seem to flip between the need for physical and non physical interaction.

About 65% of children fall into the first category, 20% into the second and 15% into the third. A more recent study has added a fourth category, **Disorganized.** Here children show contradictory behaviors i.e. Extending arms for a cuddle whilst not wanting to be picked up. It was found that, perhaps 10% of children fitted into this category (Main & Soloman 1986). From this behaviour will develop parenting styles

Parenting Styles

Parenting is an interactive process between the infant the prime care giver and thus, it is also essential to look at how the prime care giver reacts to the child. Prime care givers of the first category appeared to respond promptly when the baby cried, behaved affectionately when they picked up the baby. They also tailored their responses to the baby's needs (Clarke Stewart 1973)

In contrast mothers of the insecurely attached children responded according to their own moods rather than according to the needs of the child. Cuddles were given when they felt like it, rather than when the child fretted. The care givers of the fourth category, like their children, have mixed responses to the child. However, not all developmental psychologists agree with these findings. The whole debate is similar to the chicken and egg which comes first? Is it the child's behaviour that affects the care giver or visa versa. Some longitudinal studies are showing that parenting patterns may run in families. Thus, where parenting is historically poor it becomes essential to developing parenting classes if such patterns are to be changed.

Other research has concentrated on the opposite episodes to that of Ainsworth. You will recall that Ainsworth looked at what happens when the mother rejoins the child and not when she leaves. Frodi (1985) looked at how the child reacted when the mother left. The research found that the child's temperament had influence on the former but not the later. Babies with easy temperaments typically were not distressed when the mother left and greeted her happily when she returned. Children of difficult temperaments tended to cry when the mother left and on her return sought her out and demonstrated clinging behaviour, not letting her go or wander far from her.

This relationship between care giver and child seems to be relatively enduring and colors the whole of their relationship together. As can be anticipated, category one provides the most stable of relationships whilst three provides a very weak bond between mother and child. (Main 1988). However, some studies have demonstrated that where one parent has a poor bonding with the child another adult, usually the father, will have a better bonding. This then compensates for the lack with the mother. This, however, begs the question what happens when there is poor bonding with the mother and no secondary care giver? It has been found in these circumstances that the behaviour that we discussed at the beginning becomes more evident. Such children have difficulty in socially bonding with others, are often aggressive and socially dysfunctional.

This might seem rather depressing, but research has shown (Thompson 1982) that these parental approaches and the child's response are not permanent. If a family experiences major changes for the better or worse these will have an effect both on the parent and the child. Stress reduction or increase will affect the parents response to the child and, thus, the child will respond. The introduction of a permanent secondary carer with whom the child relates well will change behaviour. This change does not necessarily depend on gender: male/ male or female / female relationships seem to have the same effect as male female relationships.

These and similar studies suggest that children who are securely attached by the time they enter their second year are better equipped to cope with new experiences. However, it is not certain that the quality of early attachment is directly responsible for their later competence in social settings. This seems to depend more on the relationship the child has with it's parents at the time. It may also have something to do with the social pressure the child comes under from their piers.

The assumption from the above is that mother is the prime care giver and the child is cared for her for the majority of the time in the early years. In this day and age this is not usually the case. It is very rare for a mother not to be working. It is also common to find single parent families and single children. The parent is also not living near the grand parents. What this has done is to push the development of nurseries and Kindergartens where day care provision for such children can be provided. What effect does this have on the child's social development? Two schools of thought have developed each citing it's own research to back up their arguments.

In the anti day care corner is Jay Belsky (1986) who has published research suggesting that day care has a negative effect on children's development. His research points to the fact that infants who receive more than 20 hours of non maternal care per week are more likely to be classified as insecurely attached to their mothers in the strange situation task, less compliant in meeting adults demands and more aggressive in interactions with their peers. In the Pro day care corner is the Early Child Care Network who commissioned their own research (1996 -1997). They found that children who spent 30 hours in child care were indistinguishable from children who spent less than 10 hours in comparable circumstances.

What both agreed was that the quality of the service provided had a major impact on the children. Where the care givers in the day care were poorly trained and had low pay the high turnover rate in staff meant that the children has great difficulty in building a bond with the staff. High quality day care plays a major role in making the children more able to adapt to new circumstances and situations. This then has a major advantage when the children attend school. They settle more easily and do better faster (Anderson 1992) It can also combat the social loneliness a single child feels thus making them more socially able(Phillips 1994)

In summary then, children are not significantly affected by non maternal care. Any negative effects tend to be more emotional, and positive effects are more likely to be social. Cognitive development seems to be at worse unaffected or at best improved. What is not so clear is what happens to children exposed to poorer care provision.

Parenting & Belief

A further factor has to be added into the parenting of children and that is the role that belief, or the lack of it, has in the rearing of children. Everyone has been influenced by a belief system and just as this affects our day to day lives so too does it influence how we bring up children. For example the Old Testament the book of Proverbs is almost totally devoted to the ways that children and parents should interact with one another. It contains such gems as, "spare the rod and spoil the child, "and "Honor Your Father and Mother". The Judeo/ Christian ethic of child rearing is for the child to be brought in a stable relationship where the children are taught to live by the rules of love and respect. However, particularly in America, where extremes of faith are found so too one finds extremes of parenting. For example, the Amish live by a very strict code of living the simple life and have no luxuries. One often sees them driving along the roads of Mid West in pony and trap. They have a very strict dress code and an ethos of hard work. It is into this that the children are taught to honor their parents and do as they are told. They must sit at table and only speak when spoken too. The rearing of the children, whilst primarily the role of the parents, is also shared by the community.

These Amish communities are similar to that of the Kibbutz in Israel. Here there is less strict adherence to codes of behaviour but still have a religious ethos and a greater sharing of tasks by the community. This includes the rearing of children. In most Kibbutz the child rearing is shared equally by all the, mainly female, members of the community. Both these communities have been studied as they offer the researcher an ideal social setting to study alternative child rearing methods. Most of the studies have born out the work of Ainsworth and others, namely where the interactions are formulaic and governed by codes of behaviour then the child often has difficulties in social behaviour in later life. In the Kibbutz findings similar to the baby monkeys were observed. It was not the feeding that bonded the child to the mother but the degree of security provided by the mother in what is called, "Quality Time" that proved to be important to the child.

In most Northern European countries the power of religion over the rearing of children has waned greatly. However, whilst the moral arguments that underpin parenting patterns, may be lost, their effects are still observable. The social code by which children are reared and the codes and conventions that shape child parent relationships are still Judeo Christian in origin. The breaking and reconstituting of families however is having an effect on who the children bond with and take advise from. Families are no longer mum, dad and who ever else. They could also be stepparents half sisters and brothers as well as a whole variety of fleeting relationship partners that the prime care giver might have.

The "reconstituted" family thus causes great problems for the church. The advise about parenting that has stood the test of time for centuries no longer seems to fit the bill. The effect has been twofold. Firstly, some religions and denominations have fought a rear guide action and pointed out that this social development in family living will end in disaster for the human race. Secondly, because parents living in this style see that religion condemns them, they see if a meaningless archaic institution with nothing to say to them about their way of life. It is a matter of some urgency that religions look at this developing social phenomena and produce a teaching that will be in keeping with modern social trends. Finally, there has been a great debate on whether parents are needed for child rearing or not between Judith Rich Harris, author and psychologist and Jerome Kagan of Harvard University. They have a web site that takes you through their debate, the address can be found in the references for this chapter.

Social Interactions

The whole aim of parenting is to produce a socially well adjusted individual who will be able to function in society and be a useful member and eventually contribute to that society and rear others to replace the dying generations. As was said at the beginning of this chapter our social environment shapes our behaviour. We are social animals who survive by co operation and co existence. What has specifically interested psychologists is the effect that the presence of others has on us and our social performance. Almost one of the first observations made in psychology was that of Norman Triplett who noticed in 1898 that cyclists who raced with other cyclists did better than those who just raced against the clock. He went on to study a whole variety of other situations and came up with similar findings. For example he found that children worked faster when someone else doing the same task was present. Triplett called these co partners "co actionists' and the process "co action". In effect this was a form of social facilitation. In the hundred years since his work many pieces of research have been undertaken confirming his original thesis. Perhaps the best know of these was the Hawthorn Study, which gave rise to the notion of the Hawthorn effect, namely that when a worker has a passive observer watching what they do, they do in such a way as to be perfect in execution.

For co action to take place Triplett discovered that several things need to be in place. Firstly the person must be skilled in the action that they are undertaking, Secondly the person much not feel inhibited or scared by the presence of others and thirdly, they need to have pride or a spirit of competition in what they are undertaking. However, other effects were also noted that did not fit in with the above. For example why did some people "dry up" when they were asked to speak publicly or go to pieces when being watched by others? Dashiell (1930) studied this effect and added to Tipetts work by coining the phrase Social Inhibition. According to Dashiell, Social Inhibition refers to the sometimes derailing effects of co actors and audience on a performance. This was found to happen when the person was not sure or confident in what they were doing. People in this situation appeared to make more errors and become self conscious when exposed to the scrutiny of others. It was also found that when undertaking a task accuracy decreased and speed was reduced. Thus interactions can be facilitative or inhibitive, depending on the confidence one has in oneself and the task being undertaken.

A contemporary of Triplett, Gustave Lebon, was also looking at coaction but from the point of view of how people behave when in a crowd. His seminal book called, "The Crowd" (1895) Lebon asserts that the crowd is always inferior to the individual when it comes to behaviour. He asserted that when a crowd, especially when roused, started to act social norms went out the window. He described the breakdown of order like a contagion or disease, breaking down the individuals moral and social sense of responsibility. Crowds often commit acts that individuals would never dream of doing.

This effect has been observed time and again, from the Poll Tax Riots of the 1990's to the Boston Massacre (which was not massacre at all just one poor man, a freed slave). To explain this behaviour psychologists have coined the term "Deindividuation". This is when certain situations can minimize the individual identity of people and thus reduce their sense of public accountability and in so doing allow them to commit aggressive or abnormal acts.

Bystander effect

In the gospels we read of the story told by Jesus of the "good Samaritan" who was the only person, amongst the many who passed by, who went to the aid of a man who was lying in the roadside after being attacked by robbers. This is the earliest recorded event of a phenomenon called the "Bystander effect". Atkinson (2003) describes this as:

> ***The effect that people are less likely to help a person in difficulty when others are present"*** P610

In this chapter of Atkinson's book he describes various events when a similar situation has happened in real life. The key study was that of Nida & Wilson (1981) who found that the greater the number of people present in a situation where others needed help the less likely one is to find people helping. Added to this in these days of litigation people are reluctant to come forward and help just in case they do something wrong and are sued.

In the main what happens is that there is a fear of being involved and this produces what is called a "pluralistic ignorance" where everybody in the group observing a situation misleads or rationalizes what they are seeing as something they cannot cope with or a non emergency. This then allows them to cope with their own conscience. However, there are those in the crown who do not adhere to the group norms and, just in the story of the "Good Samaritan" go and help. One often finds that these are people of strong moral values and who have a well developed sense of social responsibility. My own observations over the years of working with emergency service workers is that many of these would not be people who walked by but would get stuck in if they came across any situation of another person in distress.

There is not doubt that in the lives of many of these people there has been some religious input, either at a younger age or through adult involvement. But the problem is that one is never sure if this is a chicken and egg situation; was it the sense of moral responsibility that developed their religious beliefs or visa versa? Which ever it might be thank God for them. Other research has found that once a person steps forward to take charge of the situation then, often, others will come and help. It seems that we need a leader in such situations to galvanize us into action. It is at this point that people take on roles within the situation. In my experience I have often found that, say at road accidents, that once a leader is established others will assume roles that they feel comfortable with. This includes the offer of assistance to get help, provide medical equipment, control traffic, as well as crown control and assisting you with the administration of aid. It is as if they have been waiting to play these roles all their life and the emergence of a leader gives them the excuse to play the role they have always wanted to play. This quite nicely brings us on to the idea of Group Dynamics

Group Dynamics

This is the study of how groups develop and the role that people play within such groups. Groups form for a whole variety of reasons, some are brought together by others whilst others are a coalition of people who have come together to perform given tasks. Within such groups some people will be appointed whilst others may offer to take on roles. The study of a religious congregation offers quite and useful glimpse into the way that groups operate. Firstly, let us look at how and why groups form. All of us have been through an education system and been formed into groups, by year of admission, by ability or by gender. This has often been done not at our bidding but at the behest of someone else. This is termed an "Externally Designated" group where others have brought the group into being for some purpose. Often these groups are large such as a race or nation, whilst at other times they can be small and brought together to achieve some task or purpose.

The group may also be formed by others behaving in such a way as to oppress another group. For example, there is no doubt that before Hitler started the persecution of the Jews, there were many of Jewish extraction who had almost forgotten their Jewish ness.

However, the persecution that they suffered made them into a group. Whilst some hid their Jewish background, others stood up and became more Jewish because of the persecution that they suffered. The pressure from others forced individuals to make a decision and make a stand for what reason.

Another type of group is when people feel strongly about a subject or situation and find other people of a similar mind and come together to achieve some aim. These are called "Pressure Groups" and are formed to put pressure on another group to achieve their aim or put their point of view across. Once the aim is achieved or the purpose has passed the group dissolves. The bonds that kept the group together seem to weaken as the years go by. The only time that one sees this not happening is when the group has been formed through some adversity or where the group has regular reunions. Both of these events seems to keep the bonds alive and allow the group to continue to exist.

Often within groups, especially when they are large and externally designated, one finds the development of "Sub Groups". These are small groups of people who, whilst sharing the overall aims of the larger group have particular agendas that they wish to pursue. These might be of benefit or use to the group. In formal groups these could be "working groups" set up to solve a particular problem or situation. The example that always comes to mind is in the film "Apollo 13" where a group of engineers are sent to solve the problem of CO2 build up in the "Landing Module" using only the materials that are available to the stranded astronauts. In the film they come rushing back with the "Heath Robinson" devise that eventually saves the lives of the astronauts. Other sub groups form because of a feeling of dissonance. Often, if the problem is not solved, the group will argue and destroy the group or the sub group leaves and set up another group.

Despite why a group is formed, all groups need a leader. Leaders may be externally designated by the people that formed the group; through election from within the group, or evolve from the group. Whatever the means used to get a leader, there are some qualities that a leaders needs. Chief amongst these has to be that the group believes in the leader and has trust. Often leaders are charismatic and have the ability to make people believe in them and follow their leadership. They must have good people skills and be good communicators. They must also have authority. By this one means that they must have the ability to see things through and take the group with them. If at any time these aspects are lost or perceived to have been diminished, then the group may lose confidence in the leader. In such situations an anti leader will often appear. This person may be covert in their challenge or overt. By far the most dangerous is the covert anti leader. Often this individual appears at the right hand of the leader as a loyal assistant, whilst in secret plotting against the leader. The wise leader often try to identify other possible leaders and bring them into the fold because, as President Lyndon Johnson said, " Better to have them pissing out of the tent than pissing in".

Others take on other roles such as the group comic, always relieving stress by jokes and fun; the group secretary, taking on the role of organizing and monitoring the groups performance. Then there is the group scapegoat, perhaps not a member of the group but a person who the group can agree on as the person who causes all their troubles or act as a but for their own failings. No one person has a monopoly on a role but may play various roles in various groups. It is an astute person who comes into a group, defines what roles people have developed for themselves and adopts a role that is not filled. What is more likely to happen is that the new person takes on a role they have successfully played in the past. If they perform that role better than the present holder, then the role becomes theirs. This will then lead to some conflict between the two role players and will either see them sharing and assisting each other or the development of conflict, and possibly one leaving the group.

Readers Activity

Think of a group that you have belonged to

1) Try to define what sort of group it was

2) What type of leader you had

3) What roles people played within the group

4) What role you played in that group

Compliance & Obedience

Whilst in groups we may find that we do not always agree with what the group as a whole are doing. Sometimes we go along with the group, even though we do not agree with the line of action. However, at some times we may find that we do not agree and will not confirm to the majority view of the group. Where an individual is at odds with the group often the group will put pressure on the individual. The need for conformity in a group is essential for the good working of the group. How that pressure affects the individual was studied by Asch (1958). His findings astonished most people at the time because he found that we can be so pressured by group members to go along with group action and behaviour, even when we know it to be wrong.

Asch thought that this was not conformity, for this means submitting to the group will both in body and mind, What he observed was compliance, namely that the individual went along with the group but not actually changing one's mind as to the validity of the individual action. Pressure to conform grows with the degree of unanimity that the group has over a given subject. More recent work has demonstrated that it is almost possible to produce a formula as to how a groups compliance will diminish with the number of people who object. Ross(1976) for example found that it did not matter who the dissenter was but rather the number of descanters. If only one person dissented then the compliance of the group fell by as much as 30%. This raises the intriguing question as to why it is that we feel the need to conform so readily.

Sometimes we find ourselves in situations where we do not know how to behave. Often this is in novel situations, such as a different social setting. A good example is going to church for the first time, or to the theatre. One Christmas we had a service in the church I attend which was mainly the children attending the nursery attached to the church performing a Nativity play. Few of the parents had a history of attending church and, thus, did not know how to behave when such things as prayers and public speaking were going on. The only reference that they seemed to have was that behaviour that they used when watching other performances such as those on T.V. Whilst the children performed the parents chatted; whilst the minister read and talked they wandered around, undressing the children from their costumes and talked at ordinary volume to their fellow parents. The reason for perceived intolerable behaviour amongst the non church goers was that the regular worshippers who knew how to behave were almost lost in the numbers of visiting parents. The following year the minister instructed the parents in the social etiquette of church worship, i.e. "now please stand" and" we quietly sit and hear the reading" and all complied. At other times we find that we comply simply because we want to fit in. We go along to get along. Asch found that age plays a very important part in our need to conform. The older we get the less we see the need to conform. The need to be liked and loved seems to diminished with age and one often finds people in their 70's being labeled eccentric due to their noncompliant behaviour.

However, whilst the older we get the less we feel the need to conform, we become more conservative and are willing to challenge authority. As we saw earlier with Milgrams, experiments we tend to comply with authority in our early and middle years. Teenage years have often been seen as a time to challenge authority. Shakespeare often talks about the rebellion of youth in his plays. What has been less observed has been the challenge to authority from the elderly. This may well be because the elderly, over 75, were in years past such a small group. With an increasingly aging population and life expectancy being longer one finds more elderly people being rebellious. Good examples of this in the U.K have been the ways in which the elderly have challenged the large rises in Council tax over the past few years. There are growing numbers of elderly people taking part in protest actions and being arrested for breaching the peace. Indeed there has been such a rise in the number of elderly people in prison that the prison authorities have been forced to build a prison especially for aging prisoners.

Group Norms and Beliefs

Key to a group sticking together and working effectively is the idea of having some standard norms and beliefs that bind them together. For example, members of a church have a basis common belief in God and in Jesus Christ. This belief is what caused them to come together. Superimposed on this are beliefs about how worship should take place and these then allow the group to have a set of normative behaviors that constitute how worship should be conducted. The effect of these beliefs and norms are to make the bonds with the group members strong and to make the working of the group easy. At times these norms might be challenged and the group will be asked to discussions about what they want to accept or reject. A decision making process is entered into which usually results in a common response being adopted. However, in some cases a challenge can result in schism in the group. Wetherell (1987) found that such schisms are more likely to occur when they are proposed by an individual who is not necessarily one of the leaders . However, the member needs to be relatively popular if a following is to be gained for the change. Generally groups do not like change and there is a certain comfort in having norms that are relatively unchanging. This conformity to norms and beliefs often results in what could be described as "Groupthink"

"Groupthink" is a type of thinking found amongst very cohesive groups where members want to reach some common view point on specific issues. Often this "groupthink" produces decisions that are not based on logic or logical thought but out of a need to find consensus. This often lead to faulty decision making which in the end had an adverse effect on the group. Janis (1982) found that "groupthink" occurs when the following conditions are present:

When the group is very cohesive
When the group has little contact with quality sources of information
When the group leader is clearly in favour of a certain course of action
When the decision is made under stress and in a hurry
When there is a common ideology amongst the members

What this tends to show is that dissention in a group is in fact a good thing. However, if left unchecked it could destroy the group. Thus, a group will constantly be working to reduce conflict within it's ranks. This is often achieved by good leadership. In particular where the leader takes on the role of conflict resolution by bringing the various factions together and not taking sides.

Sometimes this is not enough and accommodation between the two groups cannot be achieved. In such cases of polarisation within a group the group has a choice to live with this dissent or reject it and expel the members who hold the dissenting views. In the case of the former, bonds within the group are often found to be weakened and the group then seems to suffer from a series of minor skirmishes thereafter. In the later the expulsion of the dissenting group, whilst extremely painful to go through, often leaves the group smaller in size and very shaken but, in the long run, stronger and more able to withstand future assaults. In truth what normally happens is the leaders tries to accommodate the dissenting members but when this fails they are asked to leave.

In church life schisms have been very common both in the denominational and local setting. Being good Christians, accommodation is often the normal way that schism is attempted to be resolved. Rarely has it succeeded and often the result is a splintering of the church. What is remarkable is that Jesus gives a warning of such things happening and gives clear advise as to what needs to be done in these circumstances:-

If the vine is diseased, for the sake of the whole vine, cut of the diseased part and through it into the fire.

Summary

WE have seen that the social environment in which we develop and operate have a huge impact on our behaviour in society. Our upbringing and our faith have a major impact on how we behave in society. We saw that this process starts from the very beginning of our life on the day we are born and is a lifelong process. We are the product of our upbringing and social interactions about which faith has a lot to say and to do

References:

Harlow & Harlow (1969)Effects of various mother-infant relationship on rhesus monkey behaviour, in B.M. Foss (ed) Determinants of infant behaviour (vol 4) London, Methuen

Bowlby.J. (1973) Attachment and loss: separation, anxiety and anger, (Vol.2) Hogarth Press, London

Ainsworth.M, Blehar.M., Walters.E. Wall.S. (1978) Patterns of Attachment: A psychological study of the strange situation. Hillsdale, NJ, Erlbaum

Main.M., Solomon.J. (1986) Discovery of an insecure-disorganised/ disorientated attachment pattern: Procedures, findings and implications for classification of behaviour. In T.B. Braselton & M.C. Yogman (ed) Affective Development in infancy (pp 95-124) Norwood, NJ, Ablex

Clarke-Stewart. K. A. (1973) Interactions between mothers and their young children: Characteristics and Consiquences. Monographs of the Society of Research in Child Development, 38 (6 & 7 series N0 153)

Belsky.J. & Rovine.M.J.(1987) Temperament and Attachment security in the strange situation: an empirical reapproachment, Child Development, 58, 787-795

NICHD Early child research network(1996) Characteristcis of infant child care: factors contributing to positive care giving, Early Childhood Research Quarterly, 11 296-307

NICHD Early Childhood Research Network (1997) Familiar factors associated with the characteristics of nonmaterial care for infants. Journal of Marriage and Family, 59, 389-408

Web site: http://home.att.net/xchar/tna/ For the Harris/Kagan Debate

Tripplet (1898)

Dashiel.J.F. (1930) An experimental analysis of some group effects> Journal of Abnormal and Social Psychology, Worcester,MA, Clark University

Labon (1895)

Atkinson & Hilgard (2003) Introduction to Psychology, Chapter 17, Wandsworth, USA

Asch .S.E.(1958) Effects of Group Pressure upon modification and distortion of judgment. In E.E. Maccody, T.M. Newcomb & E.L. Hartley (eds) Readingss in Social Psychology (3rded) NewYork: Holt, Rinehart & Winston

Ross.L., Lepper,M., Strack,F. Steinmetz,J.L.(1977)Social explanation and social expectation: The effects of real and hypothetical explanations upon subjective likelihood, Journal of Personality and Social Psychology, 35, 817-829

Wetherell (1987)

Chapter 7

THE BRAIN, PRAYER, MEDITATION AND HEALING

Introduction

Long before the scientific method of modern medicine, healing was often provided through the laying on of hands and the power of prayer. Through the ages, until modern times, people have been relying on faith, religion and spirituality to bring them through disease and misfortune. Before the use of modern drugs and therapies it was prayer and the laying on of hands that cured people from diseases such as arthritis, asthma, asthenia and many other ailments.

Dr. Herbert Benson(1976) in his book "The relaxation Response" believes that prayer elicits the same biochemical response as does the process of relaxation; affecting the production of epinephrine and other corticotrophins, all of which have the effect of lowering blood pressure, reducing heart rate and respiration. It has also been found that these hormones also affect immune functioning. Other studies have shown that the relaxation response and spirituality are both controlled by the amygdala-a small structure within the brain that-together with the hippocampus and hypothalamus, also located in the brain-make up the limbic system. It is the limbic system that controls emotions, sexual pleasure, intense memory and spirituality. Thus it is necessary to explore in a little more detail the connection between spirituality and the body and, in particular, the brain.

The Brain and the Power of Prayer

Stories of the power of prayer and healing take three forms. Firstly, prayer and religious involvement can help people cope with sickness. Secondly, prayer can pray an important part in arresting the progress of certain illnesses such as cancer and heart disease. Thirdly, from a combination of medication and prayer some people have been healed. According to Dossey (1993) Prayer does have an impact but it cannot save us from physical death or guarantee we will not get sick.

Research has also shown that spirituality and religion do play an important role in the maintenance of health and healing. For example, in 1995, researchers at Dartmouth-Hitchcock Medical Centre found that heart surgery patients who said they drew comfort and strength from religious faith had the best chances of survival. Those that did not have any religious faith had more than three times the chance of getting complications. In 1996, the national institute of aging studied 4,000 elderly people and found that those who attended religious activities were less depressed and physically healthier than those who did not.(Wall 1996)

Healing through faith and prayer are very hard to study. How does one go about researching a possible supernatural event-what is there to measurement? What are the controls? Must researchers be able to measure the effect of something for it to be truly working? Dossey, author of several best selling books including, "Healing words: the power of Prayer and faith

the .. Of Medicine gives some insights as to the reason prayer may not be a very good field or research. He states:-

"When we talk of prayer we are talking about distant manifestations of consciousness.

To talk this way is to break some kind of taboo. We can accept the power of the

Mind affecting brain processes, but to talk interpersonally-that my consciousness

Can have and effect on other powers and events-is a major paradigm shift" (P3)

The Work of Newberg

Dr Andre Newburg is director of Clinical Nuclear Medicine at Neuropet Research, and Assistant Professor in the Department Neuro Medicine at the University of Pennsylvania School of Medicine. In his book , Why God Won't Go Away, Newberg hypothesis is that biology compels the spiritual urge. What science does not appear to be able to answer is the question of whether or not there is a God. Newberg says that on the one hand the concept of God is part of who we are and what we experience in our brains; however, we do have a clear answer as to whether it was put there by God or developed over millions of years of evolution.

Some of the early studies that Newberg undertook looked at the electrical changes in the brain and how prayer and meditation affected body function such as heart rate and blood pressure. For the most part these studies showed a large number of changes take place in the brain when we pray. There were changes in electrical activity in the brain that distinguished the spiritual from the normal waking states of the brain. The studies identified spiritual practices with a unique state of consciousness. There have also been a number of physiological changes noted when people pray or meditate. Usually people experience a decrease in heart rate and blood pressure, which suggest a quiescent mechanism.

The studies showed that a number of areas of the brain act

together. There are both cognitive and emotional elements involved. in prayer. The frontal lobe, which seems to be responsible for focusing or attention behaviour, becomes increasingly activated. This makes sense because prayer is a focusing activity. Another area of the brain involved in prayer and meditation is the parietal lobe; located toward the back, top part of the brain. This area is sometimes referred to as the orientation part of the brain. This area takes in sensory information and generates a sense of self. In virtually all spiritual experiences people have a loss of sense of self and often have a sense of blurring of the normal boundaries of spatial and temporal relationships. What might possibly be happening is that the sensory input that gives us our sense of self and being is blocked or decreased into the orientation area during prayer.

There are a number of other areas of the brain involved as well. These include, as mentioned earlier, the limbic system as well as the autonomic nervous system.

The Autonomic nervous system controls the automatic functions of the body and is divided into sub systems, the sympathetic and parasympathetic. In normal brain activity and body functioning whilst one subsystem is increasing in activity the other is reduced inactivity in an effort to maintain the homeostatic balance of the body. However, Newberg has found that in prayer these two systems seem to work in parallel when one prays or meditates, thus producing unique feelings in the body. People who pray intently describe the experience as producing a powerful sense of calmness or oceanic bliss whilst, at the same time, the person feels intensely alert and aroused and a feeling that they a heightened consciousness which makes them feel extremely aware of what is going on.

Such studies have given Newberg a model of what occurs in the brain during prayer and meditation. With the advent of brain imaging technologies other studies have been undertaken to see if this model has any value in fact. Such imaging studies have supported Newbergs model and demonstrated that is prayer is an active process that affects the emotional part s of the brain and some of the brainstem functions that regulate heart beat and blood pressure.

However, Newberg goes on to say that, whilst imaging is helpful, it does not tell what the person is actually experiencing. Spiritual experiences, whether they are near death or through prayer, can have a life changing consequences and are perceived to be so real that everyday experiences seem secondary. As stated earlier, this is very much due to the parts of the brain involved and the unique interplay that they have. Newberg has realized that it is important not only to have a look at what science has to say about prayer and meditation but also to take into account the spiritual perspectives of a persons experience, the reality in which they live, how these elements interact and, thus how we understand such experiences

Thus, what distinguishes Newberg's research from all others, is that he has not only an eye on the material but also the spiritual experience of prayer and meditation. Religion gives us a different way of looking at the world in which we live. Newberg believes it important to be open to all the means that we have to find answers to the big questions of life-the meaning of life and why we are here. To do this one needs to integrate the scientific and spiritual

Meditation and the Brain

To further study the effect of prayer Newberg looked at meditation. Using imaging techniques again Newberg recruited a group of people who were very experienced in meditation and prayer and brought them into his laboratory to observe brain activity as they practiced. Newberg chose a group of Tibetan Buddhist monks and a group of nuns all of whom had about 20 to 25 years of experience of meditation. Although there are a variety of approaches to meditation this did not appear to affect the study.

Newberg inserted a intravenous catheter into their arms and injected a radioactive material that would follow blood flow in the brain before, during and after meditation. As the radioactive material goes into the brain it is broken down and locks in to specific areas of the brain which gives the opportunity to take snapshots of what is going on in the brain at any given time. Newberg took a "baseline" scan of the brain before meditation and another after the monks had meditated for an hour. The second injection gave an image of what happens in the brain during meditation. This allowed the monks to mediate in the normal way. These two sets of pictures were then compared.

The results were consistent with the other models that Newberg had developed, I.e. an increase activity in the frontal lobe of the brain associated with attention and a relative decrease activity in the orientation part of the brain. The results appear to show that meditation or prayer has the same effect and uses the same part of the brain.

The meaning of Newbergs Work

The conclusion from Newbergs' work could be that there is nothing more to the spiritual experience than brain function. Others take the opposite few and think that Newberg's work demonstrate that God has "hard wired" the brain so that God can be worshipped. Newberg steers a very complex course between these two points of view. What he points out is that all our experiences have to be perceived in some way through brain activity and function and, thus you cannot rule out the brain from the experience. What Newberg believes is that all mystical experiences, from the mildest to the most intense, have their biological roots in the brain. If the brain was not structured in the way that it is, it would not be impossible to experience a higher reality. Newberg believes that evolution alone cannot explain this machinery of what he calls "transcendence" (the changes that take place in brain activity). This then leaves wide open the question of whether a higher being designed the brain so that it would be capable of perceiving and receiving the Higher being. Or did the brain merely evolve on its own into a marvel of neurons, neuronal networks, and splashes of electrochemical energy that calculate out, under circumstances into a feeling of transcendence?

There is no doubt that prayer and meditation do produce specific patterns of brain behaviour that are not seen in any other activity. What is happening is that part of the brain are behaving in ways not seen in normal brain activity. The Parietal lobe of the brain is in usual brain activity is extremely active. In normal brain scans this area of the brain would be seen as red or yellow indicating extreme activity. However, during meditation, this area of the brain shows up not as red or yellow but light blue and green indicating a sharp reduction in activity.

Newberg, as stated earlier, believes that what has happened is that this Orientation association area (OAA) of the brain has stopped receiving information from the senses in some what the information has been blocked. This led Newberg to postulate what would the OAA do in these circumstances. Would it continue to search for limits of self? With no information coming in the OAA wouldn't be able to find any boundaries. What would the brain make out of that? Would the orientation area interpret its failure to find the boundary between the self and the outside world to mean that such a distinction does not exist? In that case the brain would have no choice but to perceive that the self is endless and intimately interwoven with everyone and everything the mind senses. This perception would feel utterly and unquestionably real, exactly what the monks and nuns described in their experience of prayer and meditation.

In a summary of his research on the brain, prayer and mediation Newberg reminds us:-

That the power of prayer and meditation lies in the ability to provide the believers with experimental evidence that seems to "prove" that the guarantees made in myth and scripture are true. Rituals allow participants to taste, if only for a moment, the transcendent spiritual unity that all religions promise". We are able to "taste" this spiritual unity because of the neurological processes and because of memory associations we have in the brain which are triggered by the symbolic language and repetitive actions of our religious rituals. In short, worship involving prayer and meditation evoke feelings and thoughts associate with hope and love. Our brain is wired for rituals and that is why worship is good for us.

Near Death Experiences

In reading Newberg's work one is struck by how similar the emotions and feelings described are to those of people who have reported near death experiences. The feelings of total calm and well being; the feeling of super reality and the sense of being close to God are similar in both instances. This then raises the question as to whether the same parts of the brain are involved. But, before we look at the physiological and psychological similarities, it is important to define what we mean by a near death experience and how they are perceived.

The term "Near Death Experience" refers to a wide range of experiences reported by some people who have nearly died or who have thought they were going to die. Whilst there are many similarities in what they feel and see there is no one single experience that all have in common. However, many report of seeing bright lights, having traveled down a tunnel to a bright light and having out of body experiences. What is common to all is that such events are life changing for those who experience them. Such experiences do not happen to everyone who nearly dies or who has been resuscitated. Research seems to indicate that between 18% and 25% of those questioned after such an event have had a near death experience. In the main, the younger the subject is the more likely they are to have an experience.

The term Near Death Experience was popularized in the 1970's by Elizabeth Kubler-Ross and Raymond Moody. Kubler-Ross (1977) had become well known for her work on death and dying and described experiences that some people had that reassured them that there was something after life. However, it was the work of Raymond Moody in his book, Life after Life that really developed the study into such experiences. Moody interviewed several thousand people who had been resuscitated and questioned them on what they had experienced. Of those who had had such experiences he was able to produce a list of common experiences. These were:

Noises similar to bells or buzzers
A sense of total peace or blissfulness
A feeling of floating out of the body and observing it from above
Moving through a tunnel towards a bright light
Meeting dead relatives
Seeing a spiritual figure (Christ, angels, Buddha or similar)
Seeing one's life pass before one's eyes

Moody paints a wonderful peaceful image of joy and enlightenment in all those who experiences such events. What Moody failed to report, probably because did not fit into his hypothesis, were those who had hellish experiences. Blackmore (2004) reports that as much as 15% of those experiencing Near Death Experiences also reported adverse experiences. These have included being tortured by elves, giants and demons and seeing burning pits with bodies being thrown into them.

Studies into such phenomena have been going on for much longer than those of Newberg but the thinking and research behind them has come to similar conclusions. Blackmore(1993) states that such events are triggered by the brain state due to the cardiac arrest or possibly anesthesia. Furthermore, many people who have not been near death have had experiences that seem identical to these Near Death Experiences. These similar experience have been due to psychosis or drug induced.

Pim Van Lommel has been conducting a longitudinal study into 344 resuscitated patients to see how their Near Death Experiences would shape their lives. At the outset Van Lommel thought that if the experiences were purely physiological there would be a common experience to all who reported NDE's This proved not to be the case and led him to believe that psychological factors must interplay with the physiological. As stated earlier, Van Lommel found that NDE experiences are not confined to resuscitated patients. Similar experiences could be induced through electrical stimulation of the temporal lobe during neurosurgery for epilepsy. It could also be induced with high carbon dioxide levels in the blood such as when a person hyperventilates. Such feelings can also be induced through drugs such as LSD and Cannabis flashback experiences. It has also been found to happen after the administration of drugs commonly used in surgery such as Ketamine. However, there is one key difference between these induced experience and those of NDE origin and that is that the induced experiences seem to remain fragmentary and random whilst those of the resuscitated clients appear to be panoramic, life reviewing and life changing.

Whilst Moody is convinced that Near Death Experiences are evidence of the conscious existing separately from the brain, and thus life after death, Skeptics, believe that all of these changes can be explained by changes in the neurochemistry of the brain as the brain gradually degrades in death. Blackmore looks at some of the phenomena reported in NDE's and reports in her book the work of Dr. Troscianko of Bristol University who speculates that the noise and bright lights and tunnel experiences are changes in the cerebral cortex. Blackmore further attribute the feelings of peacefulness to the release of endorphins in the brain in response to the extreme stress of the situation and cerebral anoxia due to the sensation of breathing

Dr. Karl Jansen (2001) has reproduced NDE's with ketamine, a short acting, hallucinogenic, dissociative anesthetic. Jansen finds that those patients that have this drug administered often describe the feeling of floating or being removed from their body. He has also found patients describing other feature of NDE such as traveling through tunnels and seeing a God like figure.

Whilst neural activity might explain bright lights, buzzing sounds and the like there are some aspects of NDE's that remain puzzling. Some people, thought to be dead, are able to remember conversations between those people who were resuscitating them. They remember looking down on their body and seeing the resuscitation team working on them. As the attempts continued many talked about their body drifting further and further away from the scene. Once again, to many, such experiences convince them that there is life after death and these experiences have life changing effects on them. But do they actually see these events or are they hallucinations? To try and validate these experiences there is anecdotal evidence of surgeons writing messages on the top side of light pods in theatres and asking patients who report such out of body experiences if they saw the messages written on the lights. In the main the patients report not seeing such messages. Whether is proves or disproves such experiences as being real or not remains open to debate. Blackmore goes on to say that it is only when a flat EEG is registered and we are able bring the person back to life that we will be able to fully understand the relationship between such experiences and the brain.

The Enduring Effects of Near Death Experiences

As stated earlier, such Near Death Experience do have a profound effect on the individual. Whilst the NDE may have common features, so too does the long term after effects. Atwater (2004) found that only 20% of those who she interviews and reported NDE had no life changing effects. The majority, 80% claimed radical changes, almost as if they had become another person. Many saw the survival of death as a privilege and to glimpse what they thought of as heaven as a piece of "Amazing Grace". Many recorded a new perspective on death, no longer fearing it but rather seeing it as a door to pass through to another aspect or stage of life. This feeling seems to be irrespective of how people viewed religion and a possible afterlife before the NDE. The NDE produces excitement and illation in some, whilst in others there appears to have been bouts of long depressive illness.

Psychological Effects

Atwater has observed that it takes about seven years for most people who have an NDE to integrate it into their common experience of life, i.e. to be able to understand it and talk about the effects that it has one their lives. Seven major elements seem to be common to all who reported changes. These areas follow:-

Unconditional love. Where they feel loving towards all who they meet and find it difficult to hate

A lack of Boundaries. New frames or reference become common that govern the individual behaviour. There is a greater tolerance and more understanding about others beliefs and values

Timelessness. There becomes an increasing emphasis of living for the moment and the rejection of schedules and time to govern how one lives

More Psychic. The individual experiences more extrasensory perception and various types of psychic phenomena not common in ordinary life; having visions and dreaming prophetic dreams

Reality Switching. Hard driving individuals become easy going, Those that are materialistic dwell more on aesthetic values

The Soul as Self. Most commonly the individual talks about a more spiritual way of looking at life and how they live it.

Modes of Communication. What was one foreign becomes familiar, what was once familiar becomes foreign. Rationale of any kind tends to lose its logic and NDE's begin to think more abstractly and in grandiose terms. New ways of using language even new vocabularies develop

Atwater reports that whilst some of these changes impress some relations of the individual others find them impossible to cope with and lead to a change in the relationship.

Physiological Changes after Near Death Experiences

Just as Newberg has used brain imaging to study the effects of prayer and meditation, brain imaging has also allowed us to study the physiological after effects of NDE. Raichle (2004) has shown that such imaging has allowed us to see that original thinking uses different areas of the brain from mundane thinking. In those who have had NDE's there appears to be a paradigm shift in the areas of the brain that are used for normal thinking. Different areas of the brain appear to be dominant in those who have had NDE's and those who have not. Raichle reports observable changes in the brain structurally making the brain being more able to data cluster and towards a more creative way of thinking. This, Raichle holds points to a different arrangement of neural pathways and, consequently, different behaviour patterns. Raichle has also observed similar changes in people who suffer brain damage following major trauma.

This shift in brain activity seems to cause the person to experience visions, hearing voices and other such phenomena associated with spiritual experiences. Whilst some put this down to changes in brain chemistry others see this as possibly due to brain damage. For example, as stated earlier, it is well know that stimulation of the right temporal lobe produces visions of God, hearing beautiful music and seeing dead friends. Similar behaviour is reported by those who suffer from temporal lobe epilepsy. Reviewing this evidenced one comes back again to the work of Newberg and the question as to whether the brain is " hard wired" to experience God or not. What is sure is that we are getting closer to understanding how we experience God and religion.

Cellular Memory in Organ Transplant Patients

Whilst reading and researching the articles on the brain, prayer and healing I have been increasingly finding articles and research on the subject of cellular memory and patients who have undergone organ transplants. Leslie Takeucji (2004) has written a literature search of this subject. In her work as a physio (physical) therapist she has been acutely aware of the relationship between the brain, body and emotions in the way that people cope with pain and the whole process of healing. She was anxious to see what part memory played in the process. i.e. memory of pain and the effect it has on the process of healing. Current theory of memory is that it is a brain function and that memory cells, although not specific to a region of the brain, reside close to areas where function exists. For example the memory for doing up buttons resides close to the motor area that undertake such functions such as fingers arms and the like. Again, much of this thinking has been confirmed by brain scanning and mapping. In stroke patients where motor areas of the brain have been damaged, there also appears to be a loss of memory as to how to perform certain motor skills.

Takeuchi started to notice an increasing number of articles, mainly anecdotal, that were describing events that seemed to point to another form of memory, cellular memory. What was most striking to her was to see the number of organ transplant patients who later experienced changes in personality traits, tastes for food, music, activities and even sexual preference. Such reports seem to raise the question as to whether memory resides in other places other than our brains. It may well be, according to Takeuchi, that memory is too complex a subject to be just a brain activity and it may be part of a world of quantum sub particle systems that affects not only the brain but the body .

Candace Pert,(2004) believes, " memories are not only stored in the brain but in the psychosomatic network extending into the body .. All the way out along pathways to internal organs and the very surface of our own skin". After having discovered neuropeptides in all body tissues, Pert suggests that through cellular receptors, thoughts or memories may remain unconscious or become conscious, raising the possibility of physiological connections between memories, organs and the brain. To further support this theory two scientists from the University of Arizona and co authors of "The Living Energy Universe, Gary Schwartz and Linda Russek (1999), proposed a universal living memory hypothesis in which they believe that all systems in the body store energy dynamically ... and this information (memory) continues as a living, evolving system after the physical structure has deconstructed or detached from the body it was originally in. Schwarz and Russek believe that this may explain how information and energy from donor's tissues can be present and passed on to the recipients.

Paul Pearsall (1996), a psychoneuro immunologist and author of the Heart Code has looked at the transference of memory through organ transplantation. After interviewing nearly 150 heart and other organ transplant recipients, Pearsall proposes the idea that cells of living tissue have the capacity to remember. Together with Schwarz and Russek, Pearsall conducted a study published in the spring of 2002 in the Journal of Near Death Experiences entitled, "Changes in Heart Transplant Recipients That Parallel the Personalities of Their Donor". The study consisted of open ended interviews with 10 heart and lung transplant recipients, their families and friends and the donor's family and friends. The researchers reported striking parallels in all of the cases. The following are just a few samples from the many cases cited.

In one case, an 18 year old boy who wrote poetry, played music and composed songs, was killed in an automobile accident. A year later his parents came across an audiotape of a song he had written entitled, "Danny, My Heart is Yours", which was about how he "was destined to die and give his heart to someone". The donor recipient, "Danny", of his heart was an 18 year old girl called Daniella. When she met the donor's parents, they played some of his music and she, despite never having heard the song, was able to complete the phrases.

A 29 year old Lesbian and a fast food junkie received a heart from 19 year old woman vegetarian who was "man mad". The recipient reported after her operation that meat made her sick and she was no longer attracted to women, In fact, she became engaged to marry a man. Another amazing story, reported by Pearsall, is that of an eight year old girl who received the heart of a ten year old girl who had died from injuries received in a brutal attack. After the transplant the recipient had horrible nightmares of a man murdering the donor. The dreams were so traumatic that psychiatric help was sought. The girls images were so specific that the psychiatrist and the mother notified the police. According to the psychiatrist, using the descriptions from the little girl, they found the murderer. He was easily convicted with the evidence the patient provided. She was able to describe the time, weapon, place of the attack, the cloths he wore and what the little girl he killed had said to him. All proved to be completely accurate.

Although medical science is not yet ready to embrace such findings, there is some evidence that transplant surgery can be helped by this approach to thinking that organs hold memories. Mehmet Oz, a heart surgeon at Columbia Presbyterian Medical Centre, has invited an energy healer into the operating theatre during transplant surgery. The initial idea was to reduce the anxiety in the patient and after surgery to reduce the possible depressions that such patients often feel following surgery. The team soon noticed that there seemed to be less incidents of rejection in these patients. They were curious to see what would happen if the healer was present during the operation. Motz, the healer, registered through sensations in her own body, the emotional state of the patient during the surgery process. She felt the same with donated tissues and in so doing was able to attempt to alleviate the feelings of fear or anger or general worry that were in the environment during the operation. The results, whilst still early, have been very favorable. The team report reduced incidents of tissue rejection and increased survival rates. To many this sounds outrageous but Dr. Oz believes that it would be a disservice to ignore even the possibility that such an activity could help in the recovery of patients.

In the interest of good research there are several duplication studies going on across the USA and Europe at the moment. Few have published any conclusive studies that confirm or reject these finding, Schwarts, Russek and Pearsall are currently doing a duplication of their first study with a sample of 300 transplant patients. The questions not yet answered by any of these studies are such things as the percentage of patients that experience these changes in behaviour or personality? Do they have new memories or, with the removal of old organs are memories lost?. If so what type of memories are lost with what organs? More important than all of this is what does this tell us about other healing events.

The importance of these finding might not be self evident at first. But one needs to remember that we prior to the current understanding of the body, there was a common belief that organs did play a part in what we now consider functions of the brain. For example, love was considered to be a function or feeling emanating from the heart. Our emotions were thought to be governed by body fluids. We have saying such as, "home is where the heart is". Is it possible that what we thought was myth and fantasy might well be proven as fact?

The Church and New Perspectives on Healing

The last one hundred years have been remarkable from the point of view advances in understanding healing and medical science. The church has been challenged on many fronts from transplant surgery to genetic engineers, Birth control and invetro fertilization. In the main the Catholic and more traditional wings of the church have been against many of the developments that have been introduced, whilst the more liberal wings of the church have welcomed such developments as God inspired and, as long as they are used for good, should be welcomed. What has also become clear is that science, seen in the 1950's as holding the possibility of being able to cure all has singularly failed to do so. This has led to the remarkable resurgence in the practice Christian healing.

It is important to make a delineation between Christian healing and Spiritual healing. According to the Arch Bishops Commission on Healing in 1958, healing is:

> ***The Pastoral and sacramental ministry of healing brings an assurance to the patient that God is acting both within their inner most being and through those who are treating them. It helps to break down barriers deep inside the Personality which stand in the way of healing.***

Spiritual healing is not a Christian belief but relies on the spirit world removing evil influences from the individual and changing the aura that surrounds an individual. In so doing the person becomes who and well again.

Christian healing is more than treating symptoms. Christians believe that what is happening is the setting free of forces for health on every level of the persons physical and mental self. It is a process that restores harmony and balance within and between people. Christians believe that Jesus is the source and agent for this healing.

Through his suffering and divine power to heal he wishes all to be free from the agents of sickness. One of the treaties that he laid on the church was to heal the sick. So long forgotten this treaty has given new hope to so many. It is interesting to see that much of what was thought to be "mumbo Jumbo" a few years ago by so many is now seen to have some scientific basis.

The use of prayer and meditation are seen as being active agents for change that can affect health. Many of the compounds of oils used by the church in anointing have been found to have medicinal properties one wonders how long it will be before we find that confession and the laying on of hands will also have some effect. Where the church has made healing an almost total preserve has been in the field of Hospice care. Much of the work in this field has been pioneered in the last two centuries by committed Christian people. Hospices offer specific care for the dying in the context of Christian love. They help many through the fear of dying and death as well as supporting their families. Much of what they do is rooted in prayer. Thus the old work of many Christian communities in the past centuries meets the new world of scientific research and discovery find that, far from disproving each other, they complement each others work and prove the worth of what has been done for centuries.

References:

Benson.H. (1976) The Relaxation Response, Avon Books New York
Dossey (1993)Reinventing Medicine and the healing word, Harper Collins, New York

Newberg, A ,Aquill.D. Rause.V.(2001) Why God will Not go Away: Brain science and the biology of Belief, Ballantine Books, New York

Kubler-Ross.E. (1977) On Death and Dying, Tavistock Publications, New York
Moody.R. (1977) Life after Life,Bantam, New York

Blackmore.S.(2004) Consciousness, Oxford University Press

Blackmore.S.(1993) Dying to Live: Near Death Experiences, Prometheus Books, Buffalo, New York

Dr. Karl Jansen (2001) Ketamine: Dreams and Reality, The Multidisciplinary Association for Psychedic Studies, 2001

Atwater.P.M.H.(2004) People are Dramatically Changed by Near Death Experiences, The San Francisco Journal of Medicine, December 2004

Raichle.M(2000) The Emotional Brain, Blackwells, NewYork
Takeuchi,L(2004) Cellular Memory in Organ Transplants, The San Francisco Medical Society Journal August 2004

Pert. C (2004) Molecules of Emotion

Schwartz.G, Russek.L The Living Energy Universe: A Fundamental Discovery that transforms science & medicine, Hampton Road Publishing Company. Charlottesville.VA.

Pearsall. P. The Heart Code: Tapping the wisdom and power of our heart energy, Broadway Books, NewYork

Wall.D (1996) Aging and Religious Belief, The National of Aging, Bethesda, Maryland

Chapter 8

STRESS, LIFE EVENTS AND RELIGION

Introduction

In today world stress is seen by many as a fact of life and something that we have to learn to live with. Many think they know all about stress and what causes it and how to avoid it. However, This is not the case and much of what people think they know about stress and associated anxiety are folk law and hearsay. Contrary to what most people believe not all stress is bad, in fact a modicum of stress can be good for the circulation system. For example stress through exercise improves circulation. However, when stress is in excess then it can cause serious difficulties for the individual

So what is stress? Stress may be defined as the experiencing of events that are perceived as endangering one physical and psychological well being. Stress has two elements to it. Firstly, there is the actual event, referred to as the ***Stressor,*** and then the way the individual responds to the stressor referred to as ***The Stress Response.*** This response may be physical and or psychological. The stressors can classified as being either controlled, I.e. those we expect and can do something about, uncontrolled such as traumatic events or those that are self induced through internal conflict.

Stress and Change

Many of the situations or events that cause stress are due to change. In fact stress is synonymous with change. It does not matter is the change is good or bad either will cause stress. The changes can be perceived or actual physical or mental, all cause STRESS. In the main these changes to not last for very long, but when the do, they can cause physiological and psychological damage to the individual. However, some stressors are chronic and can affect the individual for a long period, such things as poor health, money worries or a poor environment can have detrimental effects on one.

Two early researches who looked into how changes affects stress where Holmes and Rahe (1967). They were the first to argue that both good and bad stressor could affect our health. In an attempt to measure these events they looked at thousands of lives and tried to catalogue what was happening in their lives prior to them suffering such things as heart attacks or strokes. As marriage appeared to be a critical event of change for most people they placed this event in the middle of the scale and gave it a value of 50. They then asked 400 people of various sages and backgrounds to compare other events that caused change and place them in relation to marriage. They were then asked to assign a value to each event.

This stress inventory had a major effect on the management of stress and research into it. It demonstrated that the most serious events that caused stress were, as thought, mainly negative, but also demonstrated that positive events did have some harmful effect. The scale also showed that, whilst most people reacted to stressors in the same way, the degree to which they affected individuals varied. Finally, once people realized what caused their stress it was, in the main possible to do something about it.

STRESS SCALE FOR ADULTS

In the following table you can look up representative changes in your life and see how much stress value each of these changes is adding to your life. NOTE ANY ITEM THAT YOU MAY HAVE EXPERIENCED IN THE LAST TWELVE MONTHS. Then, total up your score.

(Adapted from the "Social Readjustment Rating Scale" by Thomas Holmes and Richard Rahe. This scale was first published in the "Journal of Psychosomatic Research", Copyright 1967, vol.II p. 214. It is used by permission of Pergamon Press Ltd.)

Stress Scale for Adults

DEATH OF SPOUSE	100
DIVORCE	100
MENOPAUSE	100
SEPARATION FROM LIVING PARTNER	60
JAIL TERM OR PROBATION	60
DEATH OF CLOSE FAMILY MEMBER OTHER THAN SPOUSE	60
SERIOUS PERSONAL INJURY OR ILLNESS	60
MARRIAGE OR ESTABLISHING LIFE PARTNERSHIP	45

FIRED AT WORK	45
MARITAL OR RELATIONSHIP RECONCILIATION	45
RETIREMENT	40
CHANGE IN HEALTH OF IMMEDIATE FAMILY MEMBER	40
WORK MORE THAN 40 HOURS PER WEEK	40
PREGNANCY OR CAUSING PREGNANCY	35
SEX DIFFICULTIES	35
GAIN OF NEW FAMILY MEMBER	35
BUSINESS OR WORK ROLE CHANGE	35
CHANGE IN FINANCIAL STATE	35
DEATH OF A CLOSE FRIEND (not a family member)	35
CHANGE IN NUMBER OF ARGUMENTS WITH SPOUSE OR LIFE PARTNER	30
MORTGAGE OR LOAN FOR A MAJOR PURCHASE	30
FORECLOSURE OF MORTGAGE OR LOAN	25
SLEEP LESS THAN 8 HOURS PER NIGHT	25
CHANGE IN RESPONSIBILITIES AT WORK	25

TROUBLE WITH IN-LAWS, OR WITHCHILDREN	25
OUTSTANDING PERSONAL ACHIEVEMENT	25
SPOUSE BEGINS OR STOPS WORK	20
BEGIN OR END SCHOOL	20

TOTAL SCORE ____________________

We have asked you to look at the last twelve months of changes in your life. This may surprise you. It is crucial to understand, however, that a major change in your life has effects that carry over for long periods of time. It is like dropping a rock into a pond. After the initial splash, you will experience ripples of stress. And these ripples may continue in your life for at least a year.

So, if you have experienced total stress within the last twelve months of 250 or greater, even with normal stress tolerance, you may be OVERSTRESSED. Persons with Low Stress Tolerance may be OVERSTRESSED at levels as low as 150.

OVERSTRESS will make you sick. Carrying too heavy a stress load is like running your car engine past the red line; or leaving your toaster stuck in the "on" position; or running a nuclear reactor past maximum permissible power. Sooner or later, something will break, burn up, or melt down. What breaks depends on where the weak links are in your physical body. And this is largely an inherited characteristic.

Characteristics of Stressful Events

Looking at the stress inventory it is possible to see the three groups identified earlier, I.e. those vents that were controlled, uncontrolled or caused by internal conflict. The most common causes of stress are those that one feels we have n0 control over. In the main these tend to be traumatic events such as an accidents natural disasters or trauma to one self esteem. 2004 saw the worst natural disaster of modern times when a tsunami hit the shores of countries coasting on the Indian Ocean. In the press reports that followed this dreadful events reporters talked about the survivors wandering the streets in dazed states, totally disorientated and unable to comprehend what had happened.

These reports mirrored the finds of Horowitze (1986) who looked at how people had responded to such events as earthquakes and the like. Often these people appear to be on the verge of collapse both physically and mentally. They are unable to initiate or comply with simple tasks but do follow impassively simple orders or instructions. Similar behaviour has also been noted in rape victims who are often described as behaving like "rag dolls" sitting impassively, not thinking or responding to the world around them and even forgetting to do such things as eat and drink. In the main their attention is focused on the event and they often repeat the story of the event to who ever will listen and sometimes event to themselves.

Koss and Oesten (1998) Studied how people responded to physical and sexual abuse. Their study showed that such attacks often lead to the individuals suffering from depression and a loss of self esteem. In others there was a complete psychological change in the individual, being withdrawn, unable to manage their lives and often not liking to mix with society. Burnham (1988) found that, in severe cases, acute mental illness developed and the victim took on a personal where what ever happened adversely to the individual was always the fault of the event. This so called "Victim Culture" gave cause to what ever happened there after.

Fortunately, the majority do not suffer such severe events, however, the events that we do suffer demonstrate four characteristics, controllability, predictability, change and conflict.

What makes them stressful differs with each individual namely in the extent to which these events affect us and how much we perceive them to be a threat. In each case we conduct an appraisal as to how much we perceive these events to threaten us. Thu, it is important to look at these in a little more detail

Controllability

Controllability of an event is the degree to which we think we can stop the thing happening or affecting us. The more uncontrollable we feel the even to be the more it will cause us stress. If you look at the list in the readers\activity you will see that at the top of the list are some of the major uncontrollable events such as the death of a spouse or partner. In my experience as a minister it has been quite common to conduct the funeral of a spouse or partner and, six months or so later, conduct the funeral of the surviving spouse. This tends to happen the longer the couple have been together and does not seem to be subject to the death being expected or sudden.

Minor events such as short term conflict or frustrations in life appear to be more controllable and, as a result, causeless stress. A whole variety of studies have demonstrated that when we believe we are in control of an event or we are able to predict it's coming, the less the degree of stress it causes the individual.

Predictability

As stated in the last section, predictability also allows us to reduce the degree of stress that we suffer. As the name suggests. Predictability allows the individual to prepare for the event. A typical example is that of going into hospital for an operation. Whilst not looking forward to the event, having a date and time for the operation allows one to prepare mentally for the event. In the National Health Service of late there has been an increasing frequency of operations being cancelled at the last minute. This has been noted to cause an increase in stress and produced some abusive reactions in patients who have had their operation cancelled.

Preparing someone for a stressful event such as surgery can reduce the degree of stress and anxiety. Some hospitals have introduced a pre visiting session for patients who have not been to hospital before. During such sessions they are shown around the unit and meet the staff who will care for them. Such schemes have reduced the number of "no shows" and also appear to have a major effect on the amount of time it takes the patient to recover. Similar events have taken place with people who have a fear of flying. Several major airlines offer a "flight Awareness" session for fearful flyers. This too has proven to be beneficial.

Major Life Changing Events

As can be seen from the Holmes & Rahe list all events, be they good or bad, require the individual to undergo a number of changes in their life. As stated earlier negative events have a much greater impact than positive, but all change is stressful. Prolonged exposure to stress in one's life, for what ever cause, has a major effect on the individuals health. What effects depends very much on the physical makeup of the individual. However, there are some common physical responses to stress, These include:

Brain overstress, the individual suffers from fatigue, aches and pains, crying spells, depression, anxiety attacks and sleep disturbance

Gastrointestinal disorders, these may be ulcers, stomach cramps and diahorrea, colitis and irritable bowel syndrome

Cardiovascular disorders, high blood pressure, heart attacks, abnormal heart beat and cerebral vascular accidents (strokes)

Skin, rashes and itchy skin, changes in skin quality

Immune system, an increase in infections and neoplasm (growths internal or external)

Internal Conflict

Internal conflict refers to those events that we think about either consciously or unconsciously that have remained unresolved. These too are often events that relate to change and choices that one has to make in life. These could be such things as choosing between options for jobs, which person to support in an argument or whether to give some information that could cause trouble for you or an individual in the future. In many cases one hears people talking about having to agonize over a decision.

Atkinson (2003) talks about conflict occurring internally under four key areas. These are:

Independence versus dependence. In difficult situations we often would like someone to made the decisions for us, but are also we are told to stand on our own two feet. We also value the chance to do something independently but know that in so doing we may offend those around us

Intimacy versus isolation. The desire to be close to someone and share physical and mental intimacy but being afraid that what is shared may cause the individual to use it against one and cause hurt and upset

Cooperation versus competition. We live in a competitive world and life advances depend on competition but for things to succeed we need to work cooperatively. This results in rivalry and one is not sure if others are working for your good or your downfall

Expression of impulses versus moral standards. Every human being has impulses to behave in a way that could be considered antisocial. What stops such behaviour is the fact that one might be caught or the fact that the behaviour will conflict with moral standards set by ourselves or society.

These four areas present the greatest potential for serious

conflict. Trying to find a workable compromise between opposing motives can cause considerable stress.

The Physiology of Stress

It is only in the last few years that the full effect of stress on the brain has been understood. Modern brain imaging and scanning, together with an increased understanding of brain chemistry, have allowed us to understand how the brain uses chemical messengers to affect brain cell function. Key to this process is the Biogenic Amine / Endocrine system. To put it at its simplest the brain produces two groups of chemical messengers, those that make us fell happy and energetic and those that make us feel sad and listless. In normal living, these tend to be kept in balance and, as a consequence, we feel pretty good about life. However, when stressed, there is an increase in the production of sad messengers which distress the brain.

If the production of such chemicals is prolonged this has a detrimental effect on brain function. The individual often complains of feeling listless, unable to cope, an increase in aches and pains and a general feeling of life overwhelming them. This often leads on to anxiety, depression and a general reduction in the ability to cope with life. It appears that our ability to cope with the stresses of daily living depends on our genetic inheritance to produce enough of the happy messengers to balance the production of sad messengers. This ability to cope is referred to as the Stress tolerance.

We see these genetic differences in the way that people are affected by predictable stressful events. For example, as a young person we all had to go through school tests. Some children would arrive as school not having slept and in a state of panic, whilst others appeared not to have cared too much about the whole event. It appears that 1 in 10 people have a low tolerance to stress, i.e. they have an inability to cope with the stresses of normal daily living. Such people will live in a constant state of stress and will be subject to all the adverse effect of being stressed.

Chemical Messengers and their function

Three chemicals make up the happy messengers in the brain. These are Serotonin, Noradrenalin and Dopamine. Each has a separate and distinct function but, together, they have the ability to make us feel happy and well. Thus, it is important to look at these chemicals separately.

Serotonin has the function of regulating sleep. Located in the central nervous system of the brain is a small gland called the Pineal Gland which has the function of coordinating the chemical balance in the brain. In so doing it acts similar to the conductor of an orchestra, keeping the whole work in balance and coordinated. One function of this gland is to regulate the so called body clock which, together with the visual cues about light and darkness regulate our sleeping and waking hours. Each day Serotonin is chemically converted to a related compound called Melatonin Once converted the Melatonin is converted back to Serotonin, taking approximately 25 hours to do so. When Serotonin is high then we sleep, when Melatonin is high we are awake.

The question then arises that if this takes 25 hours, when why do we not gradually change from day time awakeness to night time awakeness? The answer lies in the external effect of light and the exposure of the natural cycle of day and night. However, some research amongst those who have no reason to wake in the morning shows that this happens. People who have been long term unemployed describe the process where their natural time for waking and sleeping gradually shift from day to night and back again over a period of a year or so.

The Pineal gland will automatically correct the cycle of serotonin conversion to match the cycle of light and darkness at the point on

Earth that the person experiences. Major shifts in earth location have a major effect on the Pineal gland and, as a consequence a disruptive effect on the body clock. With rapid travel from one point on earth to another our sleep cycle is disturbed producing an effect called Jet Lag. In the days of ocean liner sailing to the USA this effect was not experience as the body was able to gradually change as the ship sailed onward. To get the body clock back into balance with the time at the place one is at on earth takes about three weeks.

The Serotonin / Melatonin interchange also affect temperature of the body, ensuring that at night the body is cooler than during the day by up to 1C. This rise and fall in body temperature induces sleep. Most of us have experience the difficulty in falling to sleep on a hot summers night and the joy of being snuggled up in bed on a cold winter's night. To achieve the best possible sleep the body needs to be cool at night compared to that of the day. Serotonin is usually the first of the three chemical messengers to be affected by stress, thus disrupting our sleep pattern.

Whilst many people have heard of adrenalin, nor adrenalin is not so well know. This chemical has a large number of functions in the brain and nervous system. However, in relation to stress, Noradrenalin sets the energy levels of the body. Proper functioning of Noradrenalin in the brain is essential for the person to feel energized. Without enough Noradrenalin in the brain the person feels exhausted tired, and listless. People with reduced Noradrenalin production feel progressively lethargic. They appear just to sit and do nothing. They appear to on looking to be introspective and not listening to what is going on around them.

The third of these chemicals is Dopamine. This is the natural pain relief stimulator in the brain. Like morphine and heroin not only does it relieve pain it also produced a feeling of general well being. Recent research has shown. The Production of Dopamine occurs near to the points in the brain where Endorphins are produced. Endorphins are the natural pain suppressers and are responsible for our moment to moment awareness of pain. When Dopamine production is suppressed then the production of Endorphins also reduces and the person starts to a greater degree of aches and pains.

Dopamine also appears to stimulate the pleasure centre in the brain. This area of the brain allows one to enjoy life and feel good. When stress interferes with the Dopamine function the Pleasure Centre becomes inoperative. Normal pleasure producing activity appear not to appeal any longer. In severe cases of stress life can feel so unpleasurable that suicide seems a pleasant relief.

Psychological Reactions to Stress

These changes in brain chemistry produce behavioural changes in the individual. These include, anxiety, depression, aggression and cognitive impairment. Depending on the degree of stress will affect which of these changes in behaviour will be demonstrated. The most common early behavioural change associated with Stress is anxiety. In its simplest form Anxiety is characterized by an increase in the amount of Adrenalin circulating in the body. This increase causes the person to be "on edge" twitchy and unable to sleep and concentrate. In prolonged cases of exposure to stress a set of anxiety related symptoms occur which are often referred to as Post Traumatic Stress Disorder.

These prolong effects include the following:

A feeling of detachment from daily life
A lack of emotional reaction to events
Listlessness
Flashback of the stressful event
Sleep disturbances
Difficulty in concentration

A certain amount of "jumpiness"

Another common reaction to stress is anger and aggression. These reactions are more commonly associated with frustration, however, an increase in frustration can cause stress and one of the ways to alleviate these stress is to attack the cause of the frustration. Direct aggression toward the cause of the frustration may nor be possible or wise. The person may not know what to attack but feel they must attack something. When a direct attack is not possible the aggression may be displaced, i.e., turned towards something else. This could be a simple as breaking a window or, in severe cases, self mutilation. In all cases the perpetration of the act makes the individual feel a little better for a while but, in the end, the feeling of frustration will occur again and the aggression will appear again.

A juxtaposition to Aggression and anger is the apathy and depression. If the stressor continues for a prolonged period this is more likely to be the response that the person suffers. In sever cases a set of symptoms develop that have been called Learned Helplessness (Seligman 1975)

In learned helplessness the person appears to be apathetic, withdrawn and totally unable to respond to uncontrolled events. The person appears to have given up in the face of the events. Examples of this response abound i.e. when people prisoners in concentration camps few rebelled. Similarly, people who are beaten by their spouses frequently do not leave the relationship. Often they feel helpless to do anything about it because of the response it will produce in their partner.

Finally, in addition to emotional reactions people often describe being unable to think clearly as a reaction to stressors. They find it hard to concentrate or think logically and, as a result are unable to work and plan effectively. Cognitive impairment often is associated with high levels of emotional arousal such as anger and aggression as well as from the thoughts that the stressor induces. The effect of cognitive impairment over a prolonged period is to induce very rigid behaviour patterns in the individual having the effect of increasing the stress when these behaviour are challenged.

Coping with Stress

In looking at how people cope with stress, psychologists have identified two major ways that people use to reduce the effects of stress. These are Problem Focused and Emotional Focused coping.

Problem-Focused Coping is where the person defines what the problems are and then attempts to generate alternative strategies that will reduce the stress. In so doing they weigh up the benefits and costs of each alternative. Eventually the person decides which solution best resolves the stress for them individually. In the main these alternatives take the form of either things in the environment that they can change or thinks within their own personal makeup that can be altered. External environmental factors are more difficult to change than those that we have some control over, namely ourselves and how we respond to situations.

People who tend to adopt this approach to stress reduction tend to have a better control over their lives and, as a consequence are much less liable to suffer from the symptoms of stress that were described earlier (Billing & Moos 1984). This Problem Focused approach also has shown over some longitudinal studies to produce shorter periods of depression. As a consequence therapists tend to encourage stressed people to use this approach to reduce stress. Key to this approach is using the Stress Chart described earlier. The approach also allows the individual to take responsibility for their lives and reduces the possibility of developing learned helplessness.

Emotional Focused Coping attempts to stop negative emotions overwhelming the individual and thus, causing them to be unable to solve their own problems. Emotional focusing may be achieved wither by looking at changing behaviors or analyzing cognitively what is happening (Moos 1988) The behavioural approach includes engaging in physical exercise, sharing with friends or venting anger. All of these are know and proven stress relievers. The cognitive approach includes mental strategies that can be used to isolate the stressor and thus reduce the stress. These include the process of setting aside the problem and blocking it off, often referred to as compartmentalization. It can also include rationally looking at the stressor and redefining its effect to a lesser degree. Other way are by using displacement behaviors such as smoking and drinking or taking drugs, all of which have side effects that could be more harmful than the original stressor.

Emotional Focused Coping, whilst effective, does not appear to be as successful as that of Behavioural Focused Coping. Longitudinal studies have shown that those using this approach appear to have longer and deeper depressions. People using this approach appear less likely to engage in active problem solving and, as a consequence, tend to developed learned helplessness as a result Recovery rates from what ever caused the stress are poorer and more prolonged.

Stress and Religious Belief

In the previous chapter we discuss the power of prayer and meditation and their effects on the individual. Research by Moen and others over the last decade has shown that having a religious belief and using prayer and meditation do have a positive effect on the reduction of stress. In particular meditation and prayer fit in quite well with the focusing strategies described above.

Prayer works in two ways. Firstly personal prayer, asking the deity to help with or remove the stressor allowed the individual to share the problem that is causing the stress, albeit with an unseen individual. The old saying, "A problem shares in a problem halved" seems to apply in this case. In come cases the individual asks the deity to remove the stressor and in so doing start the process of compartmentalization. The problem is removed from them and placed into the hands of the deity.

The second way that prayer can be used is through requests for prayers at public worship. Increasingly in public worship people are asked for prayers. These tend to be times of sharing good and bad news within the religious family. By using this vehicle the person suffering from stress is able to share with their fellow worshippers the stressor that they have in an appropriate and socially acceptable way. The individual will derive from this much peer support.

Meditation, on the other hand, tends to fit in well with the Behavioural Focusing. By being able to take time out and concentrate on a specific issue the person is able to be very focused on this issues that lay before them. They are able to block out extraneous thoughts and feeling and focus on the essentials of the stressor. As a consequence they are able to see the wood for the trees and produce a strategy for change that will fit the situation that they face.

The actual physical process of meditation will also reduce many of the adverse effects of stress. The technique will induce relaxation and reduce physiological arousal Meditation has also proven effective in helping people with chronic feelings of anxiety, improving self esteem, and in reducing relapses into severe depression (Other studies have demonstrated that just simply resting and taking time Snaith 1998). out from life an have beneficial effect Holmes 1984, 1985). Many religious communities have known this for centuries and have offered such an experience by what is called "Retreats". As the name suggests these require the individual to come to the community and leave behind the pressures of their daily life. Retreats often last for a week or two and the individual joins in with the strict life of prayer and work of the community whilst also studying some aspect of life or literature.

Loss and Grieving

At the beginning of the Holmes and Rahe stress inventory, scoring 100 points comes the Death of a Spouse. According to their classification this is the most stressful and life changing event that can happen to a person. The longer the relationship the more traumatic the event. Further down the list one finds entries relating to the death of a close family member or friend and the death of loved pets. The remarkable thing is that in all these cases of death the way we respond to loss and grieving follows a fairly similar patter. In the process of grieving, each individual spends a different length of time working through each stage and will express each stage will a different degree of intensity.

In her book, On Death and Dying, Elizabeth Kubler- Ross (1976) identifies five key stages that grieving people tend to pass through. Whilst these five stages are always present they are not necessarily passed through in the same order. The more sudden the death and younger the individual the greater the difficulty in adjusting to the death. In more recent years further research has also demonstrated that having a final resting place for the dead person is also important for the completion of the grieving process so that the family and friends can achieve what is now called "closure". The failure to lay the person to rest delays the grieving process.

The Five Stages of Grieving

1) Denial, Shock and Isolation

The first reaction on learning that someone is dead, terminally ill is to deny the reality of the situation. There tends to be an overwhelming of the emotions and the person has bouts uncontrollable crying and may even go into shock. Often at this point the person who has been told the news is unable to comprehend to take the news in there is a feeling of total isolation from the outside world. Everything seems unworldly and unreal at that point

2) Anger

As the emotional shock of the news wears off the person starts to feel angry and the reality of the situation starts to dawn on the individual. The anger tends to be unfocused and aimed at anything or body that happens to be near at the time. The anger is also accompanied by guilt and a regret at things not done or said that could have been. This particularly true when there has been an antagonism between the dead person and those who are grieving. This may happen a few days or weeks after the initial event

3) Bargaining

The usual reaction to feeling this loss of control in ones life is to try and regain it in some way. In those that terminally ill one finds the individual trying to seek second opinions, looking for alternative therapies and possibly bargaining with God that if they become more religious could the burden be taken away from them.

4) Depression

This occurs to the change in circumstance. The grieving person feels intensely sad and find that the decision that have to be made almost impossible to do. Funeral arrangements, costings, who needs to be informed and the like all become difficult to the think about and do. Even the help from friends and relatives is impossible to cope with at times

5) Acceptance

Getting to this stage can take a few weeks or even a few years and in some cases is never reached. Acceptance comes when the changes that the death have caused become part of a new lifestyle. The person becomes calm and more organized and looks back on what has happened with a fondness for the person and a sense of closure on the life of the individual.

At times when deaths are not expected or caused through unexpected circumstances the individuals want to make something good come out of what they see as evil. In the case of where a baby dies in utero the offering of the fetus for stem cell research may offer the parents a means of making sense of the tragedy they have gone through. When a child is murdered parents may set up a trust or help line for parents in similar situations. In all cases these acts help the grieving individuals to come to terms with their loss

A more recent review by Debra Moore (2004) has reduced these stages to four and has also found that, over the years, society has put a greater pressure on people to get back to normal patterns of living. There is also a greater use of counseling and support to help people go through the grieving process. There are charities that work with grieving families to as to help them cope with grieving. When deaths occur to young children the firth thing the education authorities often does is to place councilors into the school to help children come to terms with the loss that they are suffering.

Summary

Stress relates to the experiences or events in our lives that we consider physically of psychologically dangerous. These events are usually referred to as stressors. These stressors can be traumatic, uncontrollable and unpredictable but all will have the effect of causing change in our lives. Stress also has a major physiological effect on our brain and body. Too much stress can be physically and psychologically harmful and, as a consequence reduce our life expectancy

Whilst some people see stress as challenging others find the whole thing quite debilitating. How we react to stress depends on out genetic makeup. Strong people tend to cope with stress by focusing on the things that can be changed either in the environment or within themselves. Those who difficulty in coping with stress tend to concentrate on the emotions of the events and use displacement behaviors to cope.

People with a religious belief tend to be able to cope with stress much better that those without. A whole variety of studies in the 1990's have demonstrated that prayer and meditation can have very beneficial effect for the individual. Other religious practices so as going on pilgrimages and attending Retreats can also greatly aid the person suffering from stress.

References:

Holmes,T.H. & RaheR.H. (1967) The Social Readjustment Rating Scale. Journal ofPsychosomatic Research, 11, 213-218

Horowitze.M, (1986) Stress-Response syndromes; A review of post traumatic and adjustment disorders, Hospital and Community Psychiatry, 37 , 241-249

Koss & Oesten (1998)

Burnham,M.A., Stein,J.A. Golding,J.M. Seigel,J.M. (1988) Sexual assault and mental disorder in a community population, Journal of Consulting and Clinical Psychology,56, 843- 850

Seligman, M.E.P.(1975) Helplessness, San Francisco,: Freeman

Billing,A.G. & Moos,R.H (1984), Coping, stress, and social resources among adults with univocal depression. Journal of Personality and Social Psychology, 11, 191

Moos,R.H. (1988) Coping response inventory manual, Palo Alto, C.A. Social Ecology Laboratory, Department of Psychiatry, Stanford University and eteran Administration Medical Centre

Nolen-Hoeksema,S. & Larson,J (1999) Coping with loss, Mahwah, NJ, Erlbaun

Snaith,P.(1998) Meditation and psychotherapy. British Journal of Psychiatry, 173, 193-195

Kubler-Ross, E.(1976) On Death and Dying, London Tavistock Press

Moore,D.(2004)Stages of Grieving @ www.planterpsych.com/zPsychology_101/stages_of _ grieving

Chapter 9

LINKS TO PSYCHOLOGY AND RELIGION SITES

Psychology Links

General Psychology Links

If your interests involve religion's relationship with mental (or physical) health, be sure to see what the Medline database has to offer. This is a wonderful free service!

The PsycGrad project will be of interest to people in graduate school.

Psychweb is an award-winning site for psychology resources. Psyc Site is another good psychology site. You might also wish to visit this collection of psychology aimed at high school students for an overview of psychology. If you have a psychology site on the web, consider joining the WebPsych Partnership, which strives to improve the availability and quality of psychology resources on the internet. It also has an index to the best psychology sites on the web. Self-Help Psychology Magazine is an interesting compilation of psychology resources.

Perspectives is an online magazine that deals with psychology. The August 1996 issue had three articles that you might find interesting or useful: Barb Chandler's *Can Religion Change Your Sexuality?*, *The Perception of Reality in Insane and 'Supersane' States* by Peter Chadwick, and Kevin McCarthy's *Treading or Threading Through the Moral Maze?* Stop by for some interesting "popular press" perspectives on psychology and religion/spirituality.

Mel White's Justice Net addresses questions about religion and sexual orientation. This is a very interesting page illustrating some of the complexities of the issue.

The PsychologyMatters web page offers interesting online essays regarding psychology. Several of them deal with psychology of religion.

You may find additional information from Armind Guenther's list of psychology journals, although when I last looked there, the main journals in psychology of religion were not part of that list.

Developed by the American Psychological Association (APA), KidPsych is an "online adventure" for children and their parents, including educationally entertaining games for children ages one through nine.

You might find something of value at a new ejournal called Theory and Review in Psychology. They don't specialize in psychology of religion, but they do include some articles related to religion.

Psychwatch is a useful resource for keeping informed about psychology in the news.

The American Psychological Association (APA) developed a PsychCrawler-a local area search engine-to provide rapid access to high quality psychological information. The search engine currently indexes five organizational sites that have "substantial authoritative content in the area of psychology". Enjoy!

Andrew Johnson's list of psychology links also contains information for psychology in South Africa.

PsychNet-UK may be a useful search/portal site for *psychologists* & students, particularly those in the UK.

Psychology and Religion Organization Pages

the Religious Research Association is dedicated to applying social science research to religion in an effort to benefit the religious group or its members. When I last tried this address, the site was down; it may be active now.

For excellent material from a Christian perspective, visit Religion-Online. Their sections on sociology of religion, and on religion and society, contain articles from some of the top scholars in the field.

Be sure to see the page developed by the National Chaplain Center of the U.S. Department of Veteran Affairs. You will be especially interested in their expanding section on research, which describes links between religion and physical & mental health.

A brief introduction to pastoral counseling is available, or you may wish to examine the official site of the American Association of Pastoral Counselors. An introduction to The International Association of Pastoral Counseling can be found at http://www.angelfire.com/tx2/IAPC/.

The Centre for Psychology of Religion, at Belgium's Katholieke Universiteit Leuven, is an active research center investigating psychological aspects of religion.

Here is the home of the Guild of Pastoral Psychology

Learn about the Council on Spiritual Practices.

The Journal of Psychology and Theology maintains a web page describing their work, which emphasizes a biblical perspective of psychology and religion.

The Christian Association for Psychological Studies homepage describes their organization, and provides information about their journal.

The University of Wales, Bangor, Centre for Ministry Education describes their program, staff, and research pursuits in the area of psychology and religion. Dr. Leslie Francis, one of their faculty, is an astonishingly productive scholar, and many of his studies are abstracted at this site.

The Academy of Religion and Psychical Research is devoted to spirituality and psychic research.

The Center for the Study of Religion in Public Life is an especially good source for information and commentary regarding religion in the news.

The Hartford Institute for Religion Research has excellent resources for scholars interested in religion and society.

Personal Perspectives

(Some of these are quite large and encompassing, and others are more focused. With a few exceptions for the pages that I think have something especially interesting or unusual to offer, these pages are arranged mostly in alphabetical order, by the creator's last name.)

For a European perspective, be sure to look at Przemyslaw Jablonski's Psychology and Religion Page. I think you'll find something useful there!

Visit Gene Thursby's religion pages, some of the best on the 'net!

From Iran comes the Divine Psychology pages developed by Dr. S. A. Hosseini. His theory integrates psychology and religion from a Muslim perspective.

Christine Norstrand offers these thought-provoking, and beautifully designed psychology of religion pages.

Michael Rogge is a psychologist who studies new religious movements. His perspective is quite useful and well-informed.

Dave Myers has some interesting things to say about religion. You may know him from his excellent Introduction to Psychology and Social Psychology texts. Be sure to check out his ideas!

An introduction to the Adlerian perspective may be gained by reading Philosophical and Spiritual Implications of Adlerian Psychology. Or you may want to visit the Alfred Adler Institute of San Francisco (or this mirrow), which offers a good, in-depth examination of Adler's approach.

Learn more about Otto Rank, a psychotherapist who had much to say about religion, from James Lieberman, and expert who has studied and translated Rank's work.

The Apostolic Faith Ministry is one example of how Christians apply the Bible to such areas as domestic violence.

For an analogy of the physical and spiritual worlds, see Philip Benjamin's page. This address wasn't active the last time I tried to visit. It may be available now.

Ken Hart is one of several scholars studying forgiveness, with help from the Templeton Foundation. You can read a summary of his project here.

Visit Kenneth Brown's homepage and his research page, which describes his doctoral research. Kenneth welcomes comments and discussion about his work-pay him a visit!

Matthew Clapp has established an award-winning site devoted to Carl Jung. Clapp also has developed Jung Magazine for people who take a Jungian view. You also can learn about schools that offer graduate studies in psychology and religion from a Jungian perspective at his site. Other useful Jung sites are found at http://www.cgjung.com/cgjung/linkx.html and the Jung Circle.

Diane Goble describes her near death experience and tries to answer questions that people have on the subject.

Michael Ducey's The Consciousness Project is an extension of Ken Wilber's work.

Marc Fonda's Home Page includes his thoughts on Freud, James, and others relevant to psychology of religion. This address was not available the last time I tried to visit. It may be active now.

Read a graduate student's thoughts about psychology and religion at Jay Gattis's Thinktank for the Integration of Psychology and Christianity.

Howard Gontovnick's Experiential Psychotherapy page offers a search service for people trying to obtain books or articles in psychology or religion. This address wasn't available the last time I checked. It may be active now.

My friend Howard Gontovnick also hosts a radio program dealing with religion and spirituality. If you live in the Montreal area, be sure to listen to Mind Excursions.

Dean Hammond, a religious studies Ph.D. candidate, is interested in Jung, Ricoeur, and other topics associated with psychology and religion. He's started the Graduate Journal of Religious and Theological Studies for people to exchange ideas. You also might find his main page interesting.

John Haule describes his views.

Bill Huitt, an educational psychologist, has developed several pages that you should visit. He outlines similarities and differences in various ways of gaining knowledge, describes a model for understanding spirituality in education, and offers his own views of spirituality.

Notes on the classic text by William James, The Varieties of Religious Experience.

C. G. Jung, Analytical Psychology, and Culture is maintained by Donald Williams, a Jungian analyst, and describes the Jungian perspective on psychology and religion.

Michael Kearl's thoughts on Collective Behavior and the Social Psychologies of Social Institutions ncludes some thoughts about religious institutions.

If you like to study people, you'll find Dan Mazur's "new forum" page interesting. It portrays some of the struggles of a family divided over religion. This address wasn't available the last time I tried to visit; perhaps it is active now.

Scott McDonald's page on Zen, Buddhism and psychology offers many excellent resources for psychologists interested in religion.

Shane Peterson's home page offers some links to religion resources, Catholicism, and related subjects.

Chris Phillips is a psychologist who analyzes dreams, and has developed a theory that includes spirituality.

Michael Rogge's perspective on psychological factors influencing religious movements and groups offers interesting examples of how psychology may be applied to help us understand religious behaviors and beliefs.

Earl Schaefer is doing some interesting research in the area of psychology and religion. Click on his page to participate!

Victor and Bruno Silva invite you to their Portuguese study of psychology and religion. You also may want to visit their site on psychology in Portuguese.

A recurring topic in some circles is how to integrate psychology and religion. Here is one student's perspective.

Visit David Paul Smith's homepage and read about his psychology of religion research.

Read an interview with Huston Smith.

Bill Snell is doing research on psychology and the 10 commandments and invites you to learn more about his work.

Pawel Socha teaches and does psychology of religion at the Instytut Religioznawstwa UJ in Krakow, Poland.

An interesting interview of Michael Washburn by Paul Bernstein is found in Life's Three Stages: Infancy, Ego, and Transcendence. Washburn is a philosopher who combines religion and psychology in an interesting way.

Robert Young's page includes several papers on subjects related to psychology and religion. Topics include Freud, transcendent values, and others.

New Religious Movements-Social Identity Theory. A superb examination of social psychology and religion by an undergraduate student, Andrew J. Yu. This site was unavailable the last time I tried to visit; perhaps it is active now.

An essay called "The Third Jesus" and other interesting ideas may be found here.

View the responses to the 1998 "Great American Think-Off Debates: Is Honesty Always the Best Policy?" here. I found the thoughts of Clark Berge, an Episcopal minister who suggests that honesty is not always the best policy, to be especially interesting.

Dr. M. Allen Cooperstein has written an enlightening article titled "The myths of healing: A summary of research into transpersonal healing experience". Read the article, and others from the journal Personality and Consciousness, here.

Swami B.V. Tripurari's new book examines the sacred aspect of physical love. Find excerpts from the book, as well as audio files and art here.

Read an account of one family's struggle against cancer without medical intervention. "Our church did not believe in doctors. Was our church a 'cult'? I'm not sure." View here.

Science and Religion Links

Religion and Psychoactive Sacraments: An Entheogen Chrestomathy is a fascinating place dealing with physical and biological aspects of spirituality. You won't be disappionted!

Dr. Jihad!'s Page 'O Heavy Issues includes some essays devoted psychology and religion. Follow the link to his "academic topics" page.

The Science & Spirit home page, which is part of the Templeton Foundation's work, is a peer-reviewed journal with much to offer people who are interested in science and spirituality.

View a free e-journal that occasionally contains essays on the psychology of religion at Janus Head: Journal of Interdisciplinary Studies in Literature, Continental Philosophy, Phenomenological Psychology, and the Arts

American Academy of Religion Syllabi Project compiles syllabi and other pedagogical resources for the academic study of religion. Currently, over 60 resources are listed in the searchable subject index.

For an interesting blend of psychoanalysis, physics, and religion, visit Vic Mansfield's home page.

A scholarly resource is Yale University's Project on Religious Institutions and Society, which includes a series of research papers on-line.

The General Social Survey is one of the premier surveys conducted in the U.S. This site allows you to examine some of their vast database, which includes several questions about religion.

Mysticism and Psychology Links

Some thoughts about mysticism are available at the "merovence" page.

Mysticism is also the topic of the day at Michael Foster's webpage.

Do you think that religions are more similar than dissimilar? Examine the General Theory of Religion, and Mysticism in World Religions pages. The latter page was inactive the last time I tried to visit. It may be active now.

The anthropology of mysticism webpage is now available for perusal.

General Religion Links

Overviews of World Religions

The BUBL Information Service Web Server contains a great deal of information about major world religions.

Tremendous graphics add to the information found at Mike Croghan's Religion Page. He also offers a version that accommodates frames. If you want to get the information more quickly by bypassing the graphics, use the slow link.

The Religious Research Centre attempts to show common themes among the various world religions (or click their alternate site.

Several good links to religious resources, as well as examples of using web resources to teach courses in religious studies, may be found at John Gresham's Finding God in Cyberspace document.

When I get the chance, I always try to watch the PBS show, Religion and Ethics This Week. Click here to reach their web page.

Mike Madin's excellent collection of religion resources on the internet is found at his Comparative Religion site.

A Guide to the Best Religious Studies Resources on the Internet will point you in the right direction in your search for religion on the web. Includes Western, Eastern, and alternative religions.

Worthwhile information about several religions and denominations is available from wiretap's religion gopher. The last time I tried to visit this site, it was not available; perhaps it is active now.

One of my favorite sites is Arden Eby's Religious Studies Center.

An extensive set of sacred texts, including some that are hard to find, can be found at the Religious and Sacred Texts page.

Russ Pollanen has compiled an interesting set of links to religion resources, although the site was down the last time I tried to visit it. It may be available now.

Two sites offer free web space to Christian churches in the USA, and give an index of those sites. You may find them at Houses of Worship or at ChurchUSA.com.

If you are interested in religion and you like to laugh, see what is available at Blind Chihuahua, the Virtual Church. It will leave you laughing, either with religion, or at religion.

Religion in Society

An excellent source of religion news on the web is found each **saturday** at the Salt Lake Tribune. Being in Utah, it carries the main stories about Mormonism, but it also includes interesting news and features about other denominations and religions. Check there on Saturday for interesting stories about the world of religion.

Ontario Consultants on Religious Tolerance gives information about many different religions, religion in the media, and controversial topics. Probably the best site of its kind, and well-worth your visit.

The US Library of Congress exhibit on Religion and the Founding of the American Republic is simply fascinating.

National Public Radio has done several interesting things to offer about death. This is well worth a visit!

The United Nations, through UNESCO, has interesting material regarding religious rights and the role of religion in society.

Read about sociological aspects of death and dying, courtesy of Michael Kearl at Trinity University.

Access quantitative data sets for the study of American religion at American Religion Data Archive. The ARDA concentrates on data sets not stored in a public archive and makes them available for free use.

One of the most stimulating resources for discussion of religion on the world-wide-web is The Association for Religion and

Intellectual Life's journal, Cross Currents.

The Terra Ferma: The Forum for Equitable Representation of Religion in Media and Academia invites you to help correct factual mistakes and expose biases about religion in the media and in academia.

Visit The International Association for Near-Death Studies

Information about religion and public schools in the U.S. is found at the Religion and Public Education Resource Center, located at California State University in Chico.

The Religion Report is an Australian radio broadcast of religious events and news stories. Their transcripts are quite interesting.

The Bridge Across Consciousness-Hypermedia Mirror has many interesting links, as well as archives of SSREL-L and other email list discussions. The last time I tried to visit this site, it was unavailable. It may be active now.

A National & International Religion Report is available, but the site's organization makes it difficult to use.

Read the judgment in McLean v. Arkansas Board of Education, a famous U.S. court case involving the teaching of evolution and creationism in public schools.

Some interesting views on religion and homosexuality are found at this Lambda theology site. You'll also find this essay interesting.

Religion Departments with Useful Information

You may take postgraduate MA training in mysticism and religious experience at the University of Kent.

The University of Queensland Religion Department offers a useful homepage, including a list of religion departments around the world.

The Virtual Religion Index, created and maintained by the Department of Religion at the University of Rutgers, provides an extensive compilation of annotated links for the academic study of religion.

See what some courses in religious studies are like by visiting the World Lecture Hall. You also can find information about Dr. Gerald Smith's religion courses here.

The Wabash Center Guide to Internet Resources for Teaching and Learning in Theology and Religion is a well organized guide with copious resources for students and educators.

The official site of the American Academy of Religion.

Jeffrey Hadden of the University of Virginia maintains Sociology and Religion pages including information about religious movements, religious freedom, and religious broadcasting.

The University of Manitoba's David Creamer has an informative page, including a section devoted specifically to the psychology of religion.

Spirituality (Broadly Defined)

For several different views of spirituality, laid out side-by-side, I highly recommend the SpiritSite. It is especially noteworthy for its extensive text and audio library.

BeliefNet is one of the best sites I've seen regarding spirituality and religion. A terrific resource, with something for almost everyone.

AS is an online magazine devoted to spirituality. Whether or not you agree with what you read, I think you'll find it interesting.

The Inner Voice is a magazine devoted to spirituality from a wide variety of perspectives. Stop by, I think you'll find something of interest there.

An overview of spirituality can be found at the Spiritual Teachings page. This site was unavailable the last time I tried to visit; perhaps it is active now.

The Spiritech UK site examines the intersection of spirituality and technology.

The American Religion Data Archive has recently added a new survey study to its archive entitled Spirituality and the Elderly: Survey of Staff and Residents of Long-Term Care Facilities, 1998, conducted by Bonnie L. Walker for the National Institute on Aging.

The Symposium is a spiritual publication.

Learn more about the transpersonal psychological idea that spiritual experiences sometimes may be mistaken for psychoses.

Psychiana was an approach to spirituality popularized in the

1930s and 1940s.

The Unity School is a version of Gnostic Christianity that its adherents describe as consistent with Eastern philosophical traditions including Zoroasterism as well as Christianity.

Visit TradiModern, an online spirituality magazine published in Kathmandu, Nepal.

Philosophy and Religion

The Wall is dedicated to issues of faith and doubt.

Two good philosophy sites are The Hopkins Philosophy Pages, and Philosophy around the Web.

Many good Religion and Philosophy links are found here. You also will find psychology and parapsychology links. This site was unavailable the last time I tried to visit it. Perhaps it is available now.

Visit Philosophy Since the Enlightenment, offering an accessible overview of the last 350 years of Western philosophy. Designed for "adult students learning about philosophy for the first time".

David Suiter's Religion and Philosophy Resources is a useful list of sites on the web.

Specialized Religion and Denomination Links

ATHEISM

One of the more interesting sites for people who are questioning their religious beliefs is http://www.losingmyreligion.com/. It focuses on evangelical Christianity.

An extensive resource for atheists and agnostics is the Internet Infidels.

Joel's Atheism Page will give you connections to atheism resources on the 'net, and one person's view of atheism.

Another perspective on atheism is available at Arthur Jackson's site. He also offers an alternative to traditional religion, found at his Science of Religion page.

Try the Skeptic's Dictionary to see a witty skeptic's view on beliefs.

THE BAHA'I FAITH

The Baha'i Academics Resource Library contains a wide range of material on Baha'i, including sacred writings, scholarly writings, and secondary sources on the religion.

Read a preliminary analysis of the Baha'i Concept of Mental Health

Basic information and an introduction to the Baha'i religion can be found here.

Several theses on various aspects of the Baha'i faith are available at the Baha'i Academics Resource Library.

BUDDHISM

The Buddhist Studies Virtual Library offers a wide range of Buddhist resources.

Learn about The Dalai Lama Tenzin Gyatso, the 14th Dalai Lama of Tibet, at this beautiful site.

Tibetan Buddhist monks demonstrated a mandala sand painting at Houston's Museum of Fine Arts. Read the Houston Chronicle's story of this event. Its depiction of their religion and culture is fascinating, and the pictures illustrating the story are quite good.

BuddhaNet offers an online Buddhist magazine.

Buddhists in Tibet have been suppressed and persecuted viciously; learn more about their struggle at the Free Tibet home page.

The Journal of Buddhist Ethics is available here.

The Journal of Buddhist Ethics offers a tremendous number of links in their On-line Buddhism Resources .

For scholarly discussion of Buddhism, visit the archives of the Online Conference on Buddhism and Human Rights.

An Introduction to Buddhism is another good article on Buddhism.

The University of Virginia library has established an excellent page regarding the Tibetan Book of the Dead.

The Tibet Information Network is an excellent resource for news about Tibet.

Scott McDonald's page on Zen, Buddhism and psychology offers many excellent resources for psychologists interested in religion.

Check out The Daily Zen.

Shane Peterson's home page offers some links to religion resources, Catholicism, and related subjects.

CHRISTIANITY

General Christianity

Information about Lilly Endowment projects concerning Christianity in America may be found at the Resourcing Christianity site.

Links to official (and semi-official) pages from A to W (Anglican to World Council of Churches) are available here.

The Society of Biblical Literature publishes The Review of Biblical Literature online. The RBL is a review of monographic literature in the field of biblical and related studies as well as reference works, commentaries, dictionaries, and biblical translations.

A good, selective set of links to Christian things is found at the Christian Religion Resource Page This site was unavailable the last time I tried to visit it. It may be active now.

Get information about the Society of Biblical Literature.

For the ultimate Bible search tool, visit the All-in-One Biblical Resources Search.

This site has an extensive array of Bibles available: online Bibles (KJV, RSV, NASB, NIV, Hebrew, Greek), concordances, word searches, commentaries, topical Bible, Bible dictionaries, devotionals, number searches, and even a link to over 1300 hymns to enjoy while you brouse.

Biola University maintains a searchable database called The Unbound Bible. This site is comprised of 24 versions of the bible, including a feature that allows users to compare texts of different versions.

The WWW Bible Gateway allows you to compare different versions of the Bible in several languages. Another fine Bible search site is available at the University of Chicago. This link was under heavy construction the last time I visited it. It may be available now.

The Jesus2000 page provides a good tour of the holy land.

Anglican/Episcopal

One of the best religion resources I've seen is Anglicans Online!

Brethren/Mennonite

This Brethren/Mennonite site includes general information about the Brethren and Mennonite traditions; it also provides an example of how some Christian denominations view homosexuality.

Roman Catholic

Be sure to visit Christus Rex et redemptor Mundi, one of the finest Christian sites available. It includes extensive resources for Catholics and pictures of Vatican City, the Sistine Chapel, and many of points of interest.

Examine the interesting documents at the Holy See's statement on the holocaust.

Catholic Resources on the Net can be located here at this unofficial Catholic site.

The Holy See is the official Vatican web site.

A well-organized source for Catholic news and beliefs is found at the Catholic Information Center on Internet.

Information about the significance of Mary to Catholicism is available at The Mary Page.

A group of Benedictine monks have developed a charming and useful site. Visit their Christ in the Desert pages.

Antonio Riboldi offers a new excommunication of Nebraska

Catholics who belong to groups that the bishop deems incompatible with Catholic teachings.

View the artwork of The Scrovegni Chapel constructed in 14th century Italy.

The White-Robed Monks of St. Benedict offer an interesting website that focuses on what it means to be Catholic, rather than on the extremes of fundamentalism or liberalism.

You can read a report of Pope John Paul II's views on evolution. A second version of the story is available from the New York Times News Service.

Conservative or Evangelical Christianity

End Time Ministries is a non-denominational, non-profit mission outreach.

Jehovah's Witnesses

Joel Elliott has several links to sites (both "pro" and "con") related to the Jehovah's Witnesses.

Mormon

(My special interest is Mormonism, hence the many links)

A librarian at Marshall University has established a wide-ranging page devoted to many aspects of Mormonism. He calls it The Bookman's Mormoniana Page.

The Restoration site has a collection of links to official and unofficial LDS (Mormon) material, as well as current and "extinct" off-shoots of the church. This site was unavailable the last time I tried to visit. It may be available now.

General LDS Information Resources are found at Brandon Plewe's site.

One commonly used index of LDS and related sites. (I don't like Yahoo for several reasons, but they offer this useful site.)

A selection of pictures (mostly LDS temples and historical figures) is at the LDS Art Gallery.

A collection of documents is available via ftp. Most of these will not be useful to you unless you are familiar with recent Mormon history concerning such things as the excommunication of fundamentalist Mormons, the ill-founded scare of satanism in the metropolitan Salt Lake City area, and similar events.

An electronic community of Mormons is available at the World Wide Web First Ward. This is one of the better Mormon sites if you are already familiar with Mormonism. It includes WWW Latter-day Magazine, a literary magazine that Mormons will find interesting.

Brigham Young University Home Page connects you with the Mormon church's university, which is an unusual cross between Harvard and Bob Jones Universities. Why I say this is a long story, but many of the issues are described by the BYU chapter of the American Association of University Professors. You might also want to drop by the BYU newspaper for the latest news at that school.

LDS-Gems contains tid-bits that devout Mormons are likely to find uplifting.

The official site of the LDS church.

Presbyterian

See what is happening at the Presbyterian Church USA.

United Methodist

The United Methodist General Board of Global Ministries is a well-done site that includes many useful resources and links.

New Christian Religious Movements

The Liberal Catholic Church offers a new variation on the Roman Catholic theme. This site was unavailable the last time i tried to visit. It may be available now.

Connect to The Family's web page, and see the psychological evaluation of children in The Family.

The Toronto Airport Vineyard is an interesting Christian phenomenon. Take a look.

Joel Elliott has compiled a bibliography of resources about David Koresh and the Branch Davidians.

Learn more about the International Churches of Christ at their official web site, which includes a fairly extensive FAQ page.

Information critical of a new Christian movement known as Boston Church of Christ is found here.

DEISM

A fine introduction to deism is available from the World Union of Deists.

HINDUISM

An interesting on-line journal is Hindu Studies Review, which offers reviews of books on Hinduism's past, present and future.

I have located few good Hindu sites in my travels on the web. Far and away, the best that I've seen is GHEN: The Hindu Universe.

The Free Daism page presents an interesting variation on Hinduism. This site was unavailable the last time I tried to visit. Perhaps it is active now.

ISLAM

An introduction to Islam and a Moslem perspective of other religions is found at the Review of Religions site.

The Islam Page presents basic beliefs and responses to Christian proselytizing efforts.

The banking systems of Iran and Pakistan have been transformed by Islam, and several other countries have been influenced in similar ways. Read Islamic Banking to learn more.

Answers to 25 frequently asked questions about Islam are found here.

Ahmadiyya Muslim Students' Organization provides ISLAM'S HOMEPAGE in text or graphic versions. You may also wish to visit the Ahmadiyya Portal site.

The Complete Guide to Palestine's Websites isn't strictly

religious, but people interested in the age-old conflict will find useful links here.

The Search Engine Resource to Muslim Sites and the Islamic World doesn't disappoint. This site currently links to over 100,000 home pages and websites providing Islamic content.

A Sufi perspective is found at the Sufi Path of Self- realization.

JAINISM

Far and away, the best source I've seen for information about Jainism is Jainism: Principles, Traditions and Practices.

JUDAISM

You can find a good set of links to Jewish internet sites at the Digital Genizah.

The Jewish Communications Network is one source for news regarding Judaism.

The A-Z of Jewish & Israel Related Resources may be the most extensive catalog of its kind.

Leonard Grossman offers several interesting pages. These include his list of Jewish lists, Genesis in Glass, as well as these sites for Jews in Chicago: (West Suburban Temple) and (Jewish Adult Ed in Chicago's Western Suburbs).

The Jewish Identity Development Project is the focus of Jeff Kress, a psychologist whose work is well worth reading.

Get an introduction to one of the most interesting Jewish philosophers in recent years, Emmanuel Levinas.

An interesting examination of the kabbalah is found at Bnei-Baruch's Kabbalah home page.

Have fun searching for Jewish Resources, and test your skills at a scavenger hunt too!

The Divrei Torah - Commentaries include search features to aid your Torah studies.

Shamash Home Page includes a variety of resources, including a bookstore and Hillel groups. This site was down the last time I checked. It may be active now.

Another Judaica bookstore, this one based in Toronto, is here.

The Jerusalem One gopher archive contains information ranging from art to Jewish software. This link was unavailable when I last visited. Perhaps it is available now.

Jewish Bulletin of Northern California is a superb site in a magazine format. It deserves its 4-star rating!

The premier online journal devoted to research in Jewish studies is the Judaica Ejournal.

The Vidal Sassoon International Center for the Study of Antisemitism has a large searchable database of information. The last time I visited, I was unable to search the database. It may be available now.

Tikkun makes several articles and editorials from its print edition available for you to browse.

In the Light of the Menorah: Story of a Symbol, a major exhibition from the Israel Museum, traces the history of the menorah, the seven-branched candelabrum that is both a sacred object and the national symbol of Israel.

Not limited only to Judaism, the Israeli Ministry of Foreign Affairs has several interesting resources, including historic maps of Jerusalem. You also may want to visit the Jerusalem Mosaic, which offers virtual tours through the city.

The Lubavitch movement is described at http://www.chabad.org/

Dr. Stefan Rohrbacher and the staff at the Jewish Studies Department of the University of Duisburg, Germany, maintain the Academic Jewish Studies Internet Directory. Here you will find links to academic associations, research institutes, Jewish Studies programs, and archives.

You may find the most recent Jewish news at the Jerusalem Post.

NEW AGE

World Transformation is more than new age religion, but it represents much that is common with new age thought.

New Age and the paranormal are the subjects of Man and the Unknown.

The Theosis page specializes in esoteric Christianity.

The Researchers of Truth offers an interesting view of Daskalos.

One of many businesses that will sell you new age spirituality is Quantum Quests. Note: this is **not** an endorsement of the products found at the link.

An interesting twist on new age religiousness is found at Neuro-Linguistic Programming and the Existential Quest pages, available in three languages.

Do you think that "New Age" religion is really new? Click on Michael Rogge's Newage-Theosophy pages to learn more about the movement's history.

The Enlightened Planetary Civilization presents a good example of new age thought.

The collection of new age resources at the Ontario Consultants on Religious Tolerance is very useful.

NEW RELIGIOUS MOVEMENTS

The first place for anyone to visit on your trip to investigate new religious movements is Jeffrey Hadden's Religious Movements Homepage.

The NUREL home page offers a great variety of information about new religious movements.

Michael Rogge is a psychologist who studies new religious movements. His perspective is quite useful and well-informed.

A site containing various views about Sahaja yoga and a mailing list dedicated to the same subject. Sahaja Yoga is a new religious movement run by a woman claiming to be the Supreme Goddess who created the Universe. See also Sahaja Yoga: Facts

Shinreikyo is a new religious movement based in Japan. (This group is **not** associated with the Aum Shinrikyo group that was responsible for the terrorism attack in Japanese subways during the mid-1990s.)

PAGANISM/WICCAN

Read a CNN story about witches and wiccan religious views.

A resource is available for wiccans to help people in their coven deal with psychological problems.

A pagan organization called Church of All Worlds has a page to express their views. It includes essays by members from their magazine, Green Egg.

Excerpts from the Protean Initiates Book, used at the Proteus Coven, are available.

SCIENTOLOGY & the Net

You may have heard about the Church of Scientology's efforts to censor its critics. Two sites related to this series of events are The Church of Scientology vs. the Net, and the F.A.C.T.Net 3 Home Page. If you are interested in religion and the free flow of information, you will probably find these sites fascinating.

Visit the Official Site of Scientology

SIKHISM

The Sikhism Home Page presents an interesting overview of Sikh beliefs. This site is well-worth visiting.

TAOISM

The Taoism Information Page is a fine compilation of Taoism resources. You will find translations of ancient Taoist writings and other, more modern resources as well.

Dana Riemer has several good links on his Daoism page. This page was inactive the last time I tried to visit. It may be available now.

UNITARIAN-UNIVERSALIST

The UU Association home page offers a description of their beliefs, the history of the organization, and links to other UU resources.

Another excellent site is the UU Hotlist. It has several interesting features, including a UU FAQ file.

Other Religion Sites and Sites Difficult to Classify

Bookstores Specializing in Religion

Dr. Tory Hoff's Therapeutic Bibliotheca has an interesting collection of used books relevant to psychology and religion. Well worth a visit!

Old books on religion are offered by Samovar Books, and from Dr. Tory Hoff's pages which are available here or here.

Brian Goulet offers an interesting listing of books.

SYMBOLS.com-Encyclopedia of Western Signs and Ideograms groups over 2500 symbols into more than 50 categories, many with religious significance. A fascinating resource.

The syllabi for two interesting courses on Ancient Religion are available online: Classics 330: Greek and Hellenistic Religions, University of Maryland Spring 1998; and Religion 232/ Women's Studies 232c: Womens' Spirituality in the Roman Empire and the Early Middle Ages, Bowdoin College Spring 1998.

Religion of Yoruba and the diaspora is available at this site.

The science of meditation site, maintained by Osho Commune International in Pune, India, is full of information and links regarding meditation.

The Advent of Dionysus is an online book about spirituality and myth.

The Witchcraft Bibliography Project compiles and disseminates bibliographical information about witchcraft in early modern Europe and America.

According to Professor Michael C. Kearl, Professor of Sociology and Anthropology at Trinity University, death is "the central dynamism underlying the life, vitality, and structure of the social order…(and) reveals the most central social processes and cultural values." To explain and explore the social and cultural implications of death, Kearl created this extensive guide to Sociology of Death and Dying. Throughout the sight, numerous resources to relevant thanatological resources are provided.

You can read an online book about Cosmosofy, which the author describes as a global ethics and is related to religion.

Witchcraft in Salem Village includes verbatim transcrips from trials of the Witchcraft Outbreak of 1682 that will interest historians, students, and general users alike.

Articles describing Old Norse religion are available at Viking Age.

A mix of untraditional religious ideas and psychology is found in Dwight Ott's Diagram of Conscious Life.

Information about new religious movements is available in seven languages at the Simpos site. The material here tends to be quite critical or skeptical of the groups it discusses. Another, similar site is the American Family Foundation, which tries to provide services to people who are concerned about religious movements. The AFF also sponsors a contest for students writing about new religious movements. To place these kinds of sites in perspective, you also should read the Society for the Scientific Study of Religion's Resolution on New Religious Groups.

Encyclopedia Mythica encompasses mythology, folklore, and legend. This collaborative reference resource contains more than 4400 definitions of mythical and legendary figures and almost 200 images, among an abundance of other informative features.

The primary source for information about the Heaven's Gate group is at Right to Know.

A terrific collection of links to new age, wicca, and other "alternative" religions can be found at The Portal.

Karl Eklund's unique perspective on religion can be viewed at Seeking the Third Jesus.

Learn more about Qumran and the Dead Sea Scrolls by visiting the U.S. Library of Congress exhibit.

Institute for the Promotion of Universal Theology outlines a theology claimed to apply to all people/times/religions.

The Raelian Religion site describes a group that believes in UFOs, located outside of Montreal. Related to this is UFOland, which was established by Rael, the founder of Raelian religion.

The Interfaith Fellowship tries to provide a resource and magazine broadly focused on spirituality. Articles include a wide variety of perspectives.

Information about widespread claims of ritualized sexual child abuse is available at the Witch Hunt Information Center. You also may be interested in visiting James Lampinen's page for his class on children as eyewitnesses, which includes links to related sites. The latter link was inactive the last time I checked, but it may be available now.

At the American Family Foundation, you can see an example of research based on the assumption that religions that are different are also harmful, evil cults. You also might want to look at the Trancenet site. But as you do so, remember that the Society for the Scientific Study of Religion, the primary group of social scientists who study religion, has found that there is **no reliable scientific evidence** at this time to support the claims put forward by groups like the AFF.

Ed Plotkin's Four Yogas electronic book offers a bend of Buddhism, Jung and Carlos Castanedas.

You can read about UFOs from one Christian perspective promoted by someone who prays to UFOs as part of his research.

The Alchemy Website includes a diverse range of material,

including mysticism, philosophy, and other aspects related to psychology and religion.

Evaluating Web Sites

Because the quality of information that is found on the internet varies widely, it is very important to consider the merits of the source. Here are some sites that will help you evaluate the information you find on the internet.

Evaluating Internet Research Sources

Evaluation of Information Sources

Bibliography on Evaluating Internet Resources

The Good, the Bad, and the Ugly: or, Why it's a Good Idea to Evaluate Web Sources, from New Mexico State University.

Thinking Critically About WWW Resources from UCLA.

Thinking Critically About Discipline-based Web Resources from UCLA.

Evaluating Web Resources maintained by Widener University.

E-mail Discussion Lists

The following lists deal with themes that are relevant to the psychology of religion. Some I have subscribed to, some have not, so my comments here are sketchy. Please let me know if you find any of these lists particularly helpful! The order is simply alphabetical; no ranking is implied.

Be sure also to check this compilation of internet lists relating to religion. Another resource to look at is Liszt, which enables you to search for specific topics, such as "religion," "Mormon," or "Judaism." If you have other interests, Liszt allows you to search for those too! If your focus is on women and religion/spirituality, the Gender-related Electronic Forums guide will direct you to a suitable list.

Community Psychology & Spirituality

Community psychology and religion/spirituality are the focus of this list. To subscribe, send the following message in the BODY of

email to:
listserv@email.rutgers.edu:

SUBSCRIBE SCRA-Spirit YourFirstName YourLastName

Global Spirituality Report

The Global Spirituality Report is a moderated email list that is aimed at religious people who recognize that they might gain spiritual insight from diverse traditions. To subscribe, send the following message in the BODY of email to:
MAJORDOMO@EPINET.CO.UK:

SUBSCRIBE GSR-L your-email-address

You might also want to look at the GSR web page.

Jewish-Psy

Jewish-Psy is a moderated list that is a forum for psychologists, rabbis, and those in related academic and professional fields, to discuss Jewish life, psychology and psychohistory. To subscribe, send the following message in the BODY of email to:
LISTPROC@SHAMASH.ORG:

SUBSCRIBE JEWISH-PSY YourFirstName YourLastName

The list owner is Dr. Schimmel, sschimme_delete_this_@lynx.dac.neu.edu

Mystic-L

Mystic-L is a group formed for the academic discussion of mysticism. Topics might include the mysticism of Paul, the writings on Jewish mysticism of Gershon Sholem, the work of Thomas Merton, etc. No devotional or polemical discussions should appear on this list. The list has been created for the academic discussion of mysticism by scholars of mysticism and those interested in the scholarly study of mysticism. To subscribe, or for more information, click on http://www.bhsu.edu/dsalomon/mystic-l/home.html

Nurel-L

Nurel-L is aimed at people who are interested in new religious movements. Note that this is what people commonly but inappropriately call cults. It is my understanding that this list does not condone such inflammatory and derisive language. To subscribe, send the following message in the BODY of email to:

LISTSERV@listserv.ucalgary.ca

:

SUBSCRIBE NUREL-L firstname lastname

For additional information, contact Irving Hexham at hexham_delete_this_@acs.ucalgary.ca

Psyrel-L

Psyrel-L is a moderately active list that examines psychology and religion, broadly conceived. Much of the discussion comes from psychology, but it also is reasonably well-informed about scientific psychology's application to themes of religious importance. It does not condone proselytizing. To subscribe, send the following message in the BODY of email to:

majordomo@lightlink.com:

subscribe psyrel-l

For additional information, contact Christine Norstrand at xine_delete_this_@lightlink.com

or Greg Singleton at G-Singleton_delete_this_@neiu.edu

Religion and Neurosciences

Religion and Neurosciences is a moderated list that is dedicated to how these two disciplines can inform one another. Because it is moderated, it tends to have high-quality discussions and a more reasonable number of email messages than some of the unmoderated lists. In order to subscribe, send your real name, address and e-mail address to:

lutheran_delete_this_@summon.syr.edu

Pseudonyms will not be accepted. Although you will be asked to post who you are and what your expertise is, novices are welcome on this list.

SCICHR

If you are looking for a busy place to discuss science and Christianity, especially if you want to take an evangelical view, then SCICHR is a list worth looking at. Discussion examines things like "creation science," and can be heated at times. Admission to the list is by permission only. Contact the list owner at S-SCHIM@UIUC.EDU

for more information, or look at their webpage.

Shaman-L

Shaman-L offers discussion of shamanism and shamanistic practices. It is does not condone proselytizing for a particular religion or dogma. To subscribe, send the following message in the BODY of email to:

LISTSERV@LISTSERV.AOL.COM

:

SUBSCRIBE SHAMAN-L firstname lastname

If you have questions about shamanism, you might find answers in the shamanism FAQ file.

Spiramed

Spiramed focuses on the intersection of spirituality and medicine. While I monitored the discussion there was a fairly broad range of topics. Discussion on Spiramed tends to emphasize caring and people's impressions of things, rather than what research suggests about religion. Its usefulness will depend on what exactly you hope to come away with. To subscribe, send the following command in the BODY of mail to

LISTSERV@SJUVM.STJOHNS.EDU

:

SUBSCRIBE SPIRAMED

The Spiramed listowner is Jean-Marc Mantel: spiram@netvision.net.il

SSREL-L

SSREL-L is a private list for discussion of issues like those that appear in the Journal for the Scientific Study of Religion. It is a low volume list for social science researchers in religion. SSREL-L does not welcome arguments for or against faith, nor does it welcome proselytizing or discussion of the merits of a religion or religious denomination. I have found it very helpful from time to time, and recommend it to others who study religious phenomena from a social science perspective. To subscribe, send the following command in the BODY of mail to

OWNER-SSREL-L@ODIN.BERRY.EDU

:

ADD SSREL-L YOUR@EMAIL.ADDRESS

Tantra-L

Tantra-L is a discussion list focusing on tantras, which have become part of Hindu and Buddhist traditions. The list is a closed (by subscription) list but it is unmoderated. If you are interested in Hinduism and Buddhism, you may find this list of value. To subscribe, send the following command in the BODY of mail to LISTSERV@UNCG.EDU

:

SUBSCRIBE TANTRA-L YOUR NAME

Theosci

An interesting place to discuss science and theology is found at the THEOSCI discussion list. I have not subscribed to this list myself, but am told that it is an interesting list, and not overwhelming in the number of messages sent each day. To subscribe, send the followin command in the BODY of mail to MXSERVER@ALPHA.AUGUSTANA.EDU

:

SUBSCRIBE THEOSCI

The list moderator is Gary Mann, whose address is REMANN_delete_this_@AUGUSTANA.EDU

Transpsych-L

Transpsych-L is an open, unmoderated discussion list of topics in transpersonal psychology, which includes aspects of spirituality. To subscribe, send the following command in the BODY of mail to LISTSERV@NEWCIV.ORG

:

SUBSCRIBE TRANSPSYCH-L

I have not participated in this list, so I can't comment on the number or quality of messages. If you find it particularly useful or interesting (or uninteresting or unuseful), please let me know.

http://www.psywww.com/psyrelig/links.htm-top><img hspace=10 src=

Good Things on the Net

Perspectives on People

The Virtual Memorial Garden gives people a chance to remember loved ones who have died. I was quite surprised at how well I liked this site. It is well worth visiting.

Parents and Children Together Online is a superb resource for families.

Children Now is a children's advocacy group here in the U.S.

You will find interesting resources for senior citizens at SeniorCom.

One person can have a positive impact on the world, as illustrated by the Carter Center's offerings.

For a sobering examination of the nuclear age, see Remembering Nagasaki.

People's inhumanity to each other can be explored at this University of Pennsylvania holocaust site. You might also wish to visit the U.S. Holocaust Memorial Museum, or the Yad Vashem holocaust museum in Jerusalem.

Leebert's Home Page is the funniest page on the net, if your sense of humor is a bit twisted, like mine is! I especially enjoy his list of sayings by Steven Wright, one of my favorite comedians. This site was inactive the last time I tried to visit. It may be available now.

Many interesting things are happening at PBS ONLINE®. See what public television has to offer!

The U.S. Library of Congress Exhibits give a glimpse of the past.

UNICEF's 1996 ratings of the Progress of Nations is informative. It offers a comparison of nations using a variety of social statistics.

For those of you who are teachers, I highly recommend Interactive Teacher Online.

The Wounded Healer is a good "self-help" magazine on the internet, focusing on people who have experienced various kinds of abuse.

Science

Learn more about diseases and their prevention at the Centers for Disease Control.

The Academic Resources Channel is an excellent resource for locating solid academic information on the internet.

Social Research Online is a good online journal. You may find some sociology of religion articles there.

See what's new in science at Science Daily. Other sources of science news are available from the U.S. National Research Council's Science in the Headlines, and from the Why Files. All of these sites offer good explanations of science phenomena that make the news, from hurricanes to innoculations.

The Roper Center for Public Opinion Research at the University of Connecticut provides summary infomation on surveys and studies measuring public opinion on a wide range of social, political, and economic issues. It purports to be the "largest library of public opinion data in the world".

An electronic science museum is found at the Exploratorium Home Page.

The Mad Scientist Network is a fun and informative presentation of science. Students can submit questions to professional scientists from throughout the world!

Learn more about astronomy at The Nine Planets and the Henrietta Leavitt Flat Screen Space Theater. The latter link was down the last time I checked. Perhaps it is available now.

Galileo Gallilei's life and work is highlighted at The Galileo Project homepage.

Archaeology Magazine will bring you up to date on the field of archaeology. You may also want to see the Israeli government's aerial views of archaeological sites such as Qumran and Masada.

The 1990 Census Lookup allows you to examine demographics.

View the famous cigarette papers at the University of California, San Francisco library. They offer a fascinating perspective on the debate over smoking.

Art

Visit the Louvre without travelling to Paris.

The New York Metropolitan Museum of Art will give you a view of some of humanity's finer moments.

Some people might not consider it art, but I can think of few things more beautiful than the scenery of Southern Utah. Max Bertola has a variety of pictures and articles to introduce you to this corner of the world. This link was not active the last time I checked. It may be available now.

Censorship Information

The Blue Ribbon Campaign is the most famous "free speech" site on the internet.

The File Room is a list of censorship cases, many of which involve religion, such as the Bible, Koran, Galileo and Rushdie.

Bonfire of Liberties is a beautifully-done examination of censorship in the humanities.

Computer and Internet Resources

A genuinely interesting and useful "online magazine" on the internet is Boardwatch.

Not a search site in the traditional sense, the AskERIC pages are a helpful way to find research papers on a variety of topics.

PC Lube and Tune can help you decode the technical terms surrounding computers.

If your job involves explaining how the internet works, stop by the Internic's 15-minute training series. This link was unavailable the last time I checked. It may be active now.

A good introduction to using the internet is found at December Communications, Inc.

The U.S. Department of Education has released a fascinating series of "white papers" on The Future of Networking Technologies for Learning. Read about how classrooms are being affected by the internet.

The Starting Point is just that: a terrific place to get you started finding information on the internet.

The All in One search site (my personal favorite).

Rider's World Wide Web Yellow Pages.

Find what is new on the internet by connecting with Washington and Lee University's list of new web sites, gopher sites, and telnet listings, or by connecting to the Global Internet information site, a searchable set of articles describing what's new for people like us.

Library information can be found at Exeter University's library resource page.

Looking for someone's phone number? You may be able to find it at The Switchboard.

Chapter 10

LECTURE NOTES AND GROUP ACTIVITIES

This chapter is aimed at those who will use the text in this book to lead groups studying this subject. The study notes can be easily used for presentations or lecture notes. The reader's activities in the chapters have been adjusted for use with small groups.

Chapter 1: The Study of Psychology

What is Psychology?

Psychology is the scientific study of behaviour and experience. Psychology is devoted to collecting facts about behaviour and experience and systematically organizing such facts into psychological theories. These theories aid in understanding and explaining people's behaviour and sometimes in predicting and influencing their future actions.

The study of psychology is often confused with ***psychiatry.*** Psychiatry studies the abnormal mind. The abnormal mind produces mental disorders that affect the behaviour and perceptions of the individual and, in the main, can be treated. Thus psychiatry is a branch of medicine.

The Scope of Psychological Study

The scope of study is quite vast. It ranges from understanding human development, speech and language, through how we perceive the world and learn from it, to how we remember and think. The concentration of study is always on explaining who we are and how we became who we are and how that inner understanding affects our behaviour in our daily lives.

Group Activity
At this point as the group to list subjects they think psychologist might study and then complete the list from the list below

The Biological

This area of psychological study looks at the brain and how the neurobiological processes that take place in the brain affect our behaviour and mental processes.

The Behavioural

The behavioural perspective of the study of psychology focuses heavily on observation and studying how behaviour is affected by conditioning and reinforcement.

The Social

Social psychologists mainly study how the social world that we live in affects our emotions, behaviour and our beliefs about the world and the influence that others have on shaping those beliefs.

The Abnormal

Abnormal psychology looks at what is called "maladaptive" behaviour. This is behaviour that has adverse effects on the individual or society in which that individual lives

Schools of Psychology

The Psychobiological

The psychobiological perspective believes that all behaviour has a neural basis. As the brain controls all body activity it must also control all our behavioural activity. The biological approach attempts to match behaviour to electrical and chemical activity inthe brain

The Cognitive

The work cognition means the ability to link things together like cogs in a mechanism which describes this perspective of psychology rather well. In the main it is concerned with the mental mechanisms that underpin thinking reasoning and the ability to problem solve

The Behaviorists

This perspective believes that most behaviour can be explained through the idea of stimulus and response. A strict behavioural approach does not, as in cognitive psychology, consider the individual mental processes, but rather the way that the individual responds and learns from that response

The Psychoanalytical

This perspective to the study of psychology very much lies in the developments and concepts of human behaviour as described by Sigmund Freud. Most famous for his thesis on the interpretation of dreams, Freud believed that behaviour stemmed from unconscious processes.

The Subjective

This perspective can be found mainly in the study of social development and personality. It believes that human behaviour is a result of how we see the world and not how the world actually is. We construct ideas about the world that allow us to rationalize what we see and what we experience.

Major Subfields of Psychology

Group Activity

Get the group to think of the different situations they have heard or experienced psychologists working in. List where they were and what the psychologist was doing

Biological psychology mainly concentrates on experimental work looking at the relationship between the brain and behaviour. Much of this work is done in universities.

Developmental psychology attempt to understand the factors that affect our psychological development from the cradle to the grave. Psychologists working in this field are most commonly seen in child development clinics measuring intellectual development and language acquisition as well as looking at abnormal behaviour patterns.

Social Psychology is predominantly concerned with the behaviour of groups and social relations between and amongst people. Social psychologists study group behaviour and group dynamics. This is mainly done by observation or, on rare occasions, through social experiment.

Clinical Psychology has the largest group of psychologists working in it. They are mainly found working in hospitals and clinical institutions providing treatment and counseling over a wide range of conditions. Primarily they work on conditions that have a behavioural or emotional component.

Educational Psychology, as its name suggests, looks at how we learn. Psychologists working in this speciality specifically concentrate on children who have learning and emotional problems and how learning and teaching strategies can be developed to overcome the child's difficulties.

Experimental Psychology whilst being a term that could be applied to all branches of psychology in this case, mainly refers to that work undertaken in behavioural and clinical psychology. The experiments undertaken often look at how humans respond to stimuli and how such stimuli affect the perception of the worlds in which we live.

Organizational Psychology could be described as one of the newer subfields looking, as it does, as to how people are selected as most suitable for particular jobs. This is often done by what is called psychometric testing; asking questions or solving puzzles that relate to how a job might be done. They are also involved in looking at how collaboration and teamwork could be developed in the workplace. This may be through design of the environment or how people react with the technology they have to use.

Contemporary Psychological perspectives

Increasingly psychologists are not only looking at their own field but also those of other disciplines such as chemistry and physiology to further their understanding of human behaviour and it's origins. Linked to this has been the development of technology that has allowed us, for the first time, to see the brain actually working.

Chapter 2: Psychology in Religion

The Contribution of Psychology to the Study of Religion

Group Activity

Think about the religious people you have met and see if the way they express their religious beliefs matches their personality. Make a list of the different ways people express their religiosity.

Religious belief affects our thoughts and feelings in and to every day life.

Personality type will also affect the type of religion people practice.

Byrnes (1984) states that there are three key personality types that one sees in religious practice.

"Healthy – Minded". These people rejoice in everybody and everything and feel grateful admiration for the gift of so happy an existence. They need a religious practice that is joyful extravert and very social.

"Sick Souls". These individuals often see life as a morbid existence in a world full of sin and evil.

"Twice Born". These are people who have been living a life free from religious constraints or, indeed, in some cases, opposed to forms of religion. Then they become "saved" and a new order comes to their life. They are "Born Again"

From earliest times we find that belief systems laid down codes for people to live by. One of the earliest examples is that of the Ten Commandments which not only lays down the relationship for the Israelites with their God but also how they should live one with another in their community

Such a code defines behaviour as being good, whilst deviation could be described as evil

Integrating Psychology into the Understanding of the Religious Experience

Death is often the last thing that we talk about This is because we fear death. This is reflected in the way that we treat the dead. In most religions the dead body is seen as unclean and untouchable and some rite of purification is needed to be performed

People are frightened of dying alone. This has a knock on effect about where people want to die. In the United Kingdom about half of all deaths take place in hospital or nursing homes.. Most people, when asked, would prefer to die at home with their family and friends around them.

Oman & Reed (1998) have conducted quite a few longitudinal studies into states of physical and mental health between those with a belief in a "hereafter" and those without. These studies, conducted over many years, have found that religious people are happier and healthier than non religious people. Actively religious people show lower mortality rates from a variety of diseases than non religious people.

Such findings are also reflected in the links between mental health and religious belief. Holding a belief in the afterlife reduces panic attacks and anxiety, particularly when these are as a result of the fear of death.

Another religious concept that has a psychological significance is that of saintliness. Many psychological theorists, whilst not using the term saintliness have talked about achieving a state of self fulfillment or "self actualization" as in Maslow's hierarchy of needs. The result of this is often seen as an inner calm and a sense of love and good will to the world.

As part of our human condition we all need people to look up to and roll models to follow. Whilst in the past this was the roll of the saints, today it is the roll of the pop idol or fashion guru.

Religious Experience from the Psychological Perspective

Byrnes, (1984) describes three attributes thc religious experience.

Firstly **Ineffability**. It is only when one meets with another person who has had a similar experience that one can share the experience and perceive it's reality to the individuals.

Secondly **Transiency**. These mystical states brought on by religious fervor are brief and quickly pass. They are so powerful in the individual that they cannot be sustained for long.

Thirdly, **Passivity**. This state can be encouraged by preparation such as meditation or the performance of a physical task but, in the main people who have a religious experience talk about a powerlessness of their will to cause the feelings to happen.

Whilst it is true that these mystical experiences are mainly found in the lives of the religious, they are not exclusive. They can also be found when listening to music or reading poetry.

Group Activity

Think about the way you pray.
Make a list of the different types

of prayer you use and in what situations you have used them. Write a few words on what are the effects of prayer for you, and then share with the group

Prayer requires the individual to believe that a) they have the ability to commune with their God and b) that this God listens and has the ability to respond.

During the devotional experience the individual is in complete control of their consciousness.

For many prayer allows the individual to share with their God the concerns, worries and fears that they have. Few people actually pray in any great depth thanking God or expressing joy. Most people pray when there is a crisis in their lives. As a consequence it can be seen as a coping mechanism to deal with anxiety and stress

Psychologists have long studied the ways that people cope with stress. Several strategies have been observed that have some relationship to prayer. In most strategies the first step is to clearly define the problem. By taking time out and sitting or kneeling this often allows the individual to focus on what the problem actually is.

Another strategy is to engage in focusing on the emotions created by anxiety and stress so as to stop them overwhelming the individual. This strategy can be divided into two types of displacement behaviors. The first is physical, where the individual may engage in physical activity to lessen the stress, i.e. positively by taking part in physical exercise or negatively by drinking excessively or taking drugs. The second is by indulging in cognitive activity (thinking) which helps to reduce the threat.

It has been found that prayer plays an important psychological role in allowing us to cope with the strains and stresses of everyday life.

Some researchers point to the fact that for prayer to work, the individual has to have an active imagination. This is deemed to be essential. For the individual needs to be able to imagine the god they are talking to.

What all this points to is that an understanding of psychology can help in the understanding of why humans need religion and the effects that this has on our lives. Newburg states that if we did not already have religions in the world we would have to invent them to fulfill a human need. This can be born out by looking at anthropology studies which demonstrate that in all human settlements across all the world there has some form of god worship. Religion is fundamental to human behaviour and the control of it fundamental to religion.

Chapter 3: Personality Development & Religion

What is Personality?

Personality can be defined as:

The distinctive and characteristic patterns of thought, emotion and

Behaviour that make up an individual's personal style of interacting

With the physical and social environment.

In trying to study Personality, psychologists have devised a whole series of theories as to how it develops. Psychologists have long argued as to whether it is something that is inborn (innate) or something we develop as a reaction to our environment whilst growing up.

In the earliest studies of Personality **Allport & Odbert** resorted to looking in the dictionary to find words that described, in their view, traits of behaviour. In this laborious study they found nearly 18.000 words that described some trait of personality. **Cattell** brought this down to 200 traits that could be used to define personality. These included such traits as, openness, agreeability and sociable.

Freud, had attempted to define personality without resorting to the use of traits. To explain how personality influenced the individual they developed new words, such as the Id or Ego,

Theories of Personality

The Psychoanalytic Approach

At the outset it is important to state that this theory, of all the theories of personality, is the least scientific, and yet remains one of the most influential. Based on the work of Freud it relies for its basis not on scientific fact but on his observations whilst working as a neurologist and treating patients with nervous diseases. From his observations he developed what he called the structural model of the mind. This has three elements, the Id the Ego and the super ego.

The Id was made up of our most basic drives, such as the need for food, drink, sleep and the avoidance of pain. There was also a drive for self preservation which manifested itself in the drives of aggression and the need for sex. According to Freud the Id demands immediate gratification once the drive has developed.

The Ego develops from the Id. Carers soon teach the child that immediate gratification of one's needs is not the way of the world. The child attempts to seek gratification whilst the carer seeks to impose rules on to the child behaviour. These periods of conflict have passed into poplar culture at "The Terrible Two's" and the like. It is when the demands of the Id have to subject to the realities of the environment in which the child lives.

The Superego is the arbiter between the Id and the Ego. It judges the needs of the Id and the response of the Ego as to whether the action was right or wrong. It is the repository of a moral and social conscience as well as our ideal self. It develops as a response to the rewards and punishments that our carers impose upon us during our upbringing.

According to Freud these three elements are in constant interplay. Whist the Id demands gratification the Ego is trying to find socially acceptable forms of gratification and above these two sits the superego constantly battling with the other two because the behaviour often falls short of what is ideal. In the well balanced individual the interplay between these three is socially acceptable whilst the unbalanced of has the Id in the ascendancy.

Mental Defense Mechanisms

There are seven mental defense mechanisms They help us to cope with the difficult and stressful events in our lives.

These Mental Defense Mechanisms are as follows:

Denial

This is when we deny that an event has taken place. Often these events are unpleasant or emotionally traumatic and as a consequence they are so repressed as to be almost forgotten.

Rationalization

Here the individual attempts to explain away the events that have taken place in a more rational form.

Repression

This is when impulses or memories are too frightening or painful to cope with and, as a consequence, they are totally excluded from our conscious awareness.

Projection

How often have you had someone talk about what they see as your faults only for you to think that they are actually describing themselves? This is in fact a defense mechanism called projection. What we recognized as our own undesirable qualities are assigned to other people in exaggerated accounts.

Reaction Formation

Is perhaps the most difficult of all the Mental Defense Mechanisms to understand. Suppose a mother really does not love her child. She hides the feeling she had by demonstrating the opposite reaction. She may show distress when the child is away from her. She may become overindulgent to the child or take the child's wishes and implement them in an extreme form

Intellectualization

This allows the individual to detach themselves from the stressful situation and form an abstract theory as to why the stressful event took place.

Displacement

This mechanism allows for a drive to be directed in a different form so as to allow it's fulfillment to be socially acceptable.

Group Activity

After reading the descriptions of these mental defense mechanisms think about your own life and behaviour and see if you can identify any of these mechanisms active in your own behaviour. Then share these insights with the group

Freud's Theory of Personality Development

The pleasure seeking principle of the Id focused on different parts of the body and activities associated with them. In the first year of life infants get pleasure from oral experiences such as feeding or sucking things in their mouth. In the Second year the focus seems to change to the pleasure in excreting or withholding faeces. Around the third year until the sixth the child becomes preoccupied with the genital region. The child gains great pleasure from fondling the genitals. The child also learns to differentiate from the sexes and becomes aware of sexual impulses.

Around the age of 6 these sexual impulses in a male child tend to be directed towards their mother. The child sees the father and other male children as rival for the mother's affection. This is termed the Oedipus Conflict stage, after the Greek legend of Oedipus. Resolution of this conflict comes when the child takes the father as a role model and develops iconic attitudes towards him. Around the age of 7 to 12 the child becomes less concerned about their sexuality and more about the world in which they live and the skills needed to survive. This is called the latency stage the final stage happens is adolescences when a mature attitude to sexuality is developing and is called the genital stage.

The Behaviorist Theory of Development

This approach, on the other hand, sees the new born baby as having no real personality at birth. The theory places great emphasis on the importance of how the environment, including people and events, mould and determine behaviour from the first day of our lives.

Thus, our personality depends very much upon the environment in which we were brought up in and developed.

The Cognitive Approach

The cognitive approach sees the importance of influences from outside but also acknowledges that thought and thought processes must have an effect on personality development

The Humanist Approach

The humanist approach believed that it is the subjective experiences of our life that shaped who we are and who we become. It is the sum total of our human experience that makes us who we are. Underlying all of this is our basic human needs that drive us to achieve

This **Self Concept** included all the perceptions, values and attitudes that characterize "me" or "I". Who I am and what I think I can do will influence my attitudes and behaviour in the world in which I live. The individual thus evaluates the experiences they undergo in the light of who they think they are. This then influences the way in which we behave in given situations. This is what Rogers called our **"Actual Self".**

Rogers believed that the closer the concepts of **Actual and Ideal Self** were the happier and more stable the person would be. The further apart they were the more imbalanced and disturbed the individual would be. When the actual and ideal were the same, almost impossibility, then we would have achieved "Self Actualization" or self fulfillment.

Overlapping the work of Rogers was that of Abraham Maslow who also was working on how need fulfillment affected our behaviour. Maslow is best known for the development of a hierarchy of human needs. This hierarchy, according to Maslow, started off with a set of basic physiological needs, hunger, thirst etc. Maslow believed

needs at one level need to be partially achieved before those at another level become

important motivators for our actions. However, whilst advancing through a hierarchy

should a lower level of need become less satisfied then our needs drop to that level. At the highest point of this hierarchy of needs is the concept of self actualization.

The Evolutionary Approach

This theory attempts to address many of the questions that are age old in relation to the differences in the sexes. It has long been recognized that what women look for in a mate is different to that of a male. Females invest a large part of their time to the rearing of children and the provision of a safe and secure environment for the family to live in. Thus, she will look for a mate that will provide genes that will produce strong health children and also have the ability to provide for the family and share in the child rearing. Men on the other hand look primarily for females that are available, willing and fertile. Other attributes come well down the line.

Trait Theory

Through factor analysis Eysenck arrived at two personality traits, **introvert-extravert** and emotional stability-instability.

Introvert – Extravert refers to the degree to which and individual is orientated inward towards themselves or outward towards the world. At the introvert end of the scale the person is shy, withdrawn and likes solitude, whilst at the extravert end of the scale the individual is out going, sociable and needing company. The dimensions of **stable – unstable** relate to the emotionality of the individual. According to Eysenck we all sit somewhere in the paradigms set by these two axes. In the main the more introverted we are the more emotionally unable we become and vice versa.

How Religious Beliefs Play a Part in Personality Development

Group Activity

After reading these various theories of personality and it's development set up separate groups for each theory about a theory and ask them if they can identify how having a religious believe could play a part in the development of personality. Get them to write down their conclusions and share them with the other groups.

For personality to develop there has to be some reaction with other people. The prime people involved are the parents or carers of the developing child. Much of what these people are responsible for is the imposition of socially acceptable behaviour on the individual. In the main parents judge what is right or wrong, good or bad by how they themselves were brought up. Many of these judgments rest of religious beliefs

In some religions and culture this schooling in religious belief is undertaken in a very strict way and is left to the religious leaders to undertake. One sees this in Orthodox Judaism and the Muslim faith where schooling takes place in a highly disciplined and traditional way. Often the completion of this schooling is marked by some rite of passage that moves the person from childhood to adult life. To a lesser extent this is also seen in the Christian faith, with Sunday school and confirmation.

Chapter 4: Personality theorists and the Religious Experience

Freud 1856-1939

At the time that most of the personality theorist were writing and developing their theories religion, especially the Christian religion were still very dominant in the European culture of their day. Freud was born and brought up in the catholic culture of Vienna, as were many of the patients that he based his observations on. Freud was in fact a Jew It was only in the later years that his thoughts turned back to religion and his own faith.

Freud saw the religious experience as a projection of a father figure who had the ability to shield and defend the individual from conflicts in our personal and social life. This concept of defender was quite common in the mid to late 18th century.

In the later half of the 20th century and the beginning of the 21st there has been a major emasculation of the role of the father in the family. Whilst there are many explanations for this role softening it has given rise to what is called the "New Man". This is, in the main, seen as where a man takes on some of the role of the mother and shares in domestic duties and child rearing. At the same time there has also been an emasculation of the father figure in God. Prayers have been written addressing the Christian deity as "Our Father and Mother in God". In St. Patrick's Cathedral in New York there is a sculpture depicting God as a woman.

Jung 1875-1961

Jung was born and brought up in Basel, the son of a clergyman. From a very early age he had been immersed in religious life and thinking. It was no wonder then that he showed a great interest in theology and mysticism during his medical studies.

Jung's ideas about the structure of the psyche and the ways people achieve their potential are very much based on his view of religion. From the psyche comes the archetypes, that give us an mage of God, and thus religious faith. Some of these archetypes are almost universal to a community, for example the image of God as an old man. This Jung called this "the collective psyche"; archetypes that we all recognize. He saw that religions were mainly concerned with devils, saviors and the like and these have reflections in the thinking of each and every one of us

Jung thought that the closer we grew to knowing ourselves the closer we came to harmony with ourselves. He saw the Self as an intellectual construct that served to express an unknowable essence that we cannot grasp, since by definition it transcends our powers of comprehension. It might equally be called "God within us" (1972, p238).

Allport 1897-1967

Gordon Allport was an American from a fairly wealthy family in Indiana. According to Allport the ethic of the family was hard work and steadfast belief in God. He was brought up in a protestant home who believed that all problems could be solved if placed in God's hands and prayed about. The family believed in a "muscular" Christianity which meant that they often helped people who were in trouble. Is it any wonder then that when he went to university at Harvard, he studied psychology and social work? He said himself that he just simply liked helping people. However Allport was not immune form the influences of Freud and Jung because he spent his PhD year studying in Germany.

Allport believed that religion represented the highest form of human striving for a goal. To be religious was the ultimate in the human condition and to have a personality that demonstrated a conscience the ultimate need to attaining that goal. For Allport religion was the driving force to the discovery of goodness and religious practice the mechanism for achieving that goal. Prayer focuses faith, sometimes allowing the person praying to self reflect and at other times to concentrate on inner energies and activities that develop a godly state of the mind. He also saw religion as the great unifying force and also the drive that pushed people and communities often beyond themselves to achieve a greater good than would be possible by oneself.

Perhaps the area that illustrates best the integration of Allports theory of personality and his religious belief was when he talked about the development of the "Conscience". Unlike Freud who says this as just a mechanism for developing obedience, Allport saw the conscience as a much higher order of behaviour. In fact for him it was the goal or religious behaviour. Conscience develops as the individual matures and out of its influence comes moral behaviour. For Allport key to this process is the setting of long term goals and an ideal self image. Allport called this collective a "values schema"

Group Activity

Get the group to look again at Maslows "Hierarchy of Needs and see if they can think of how the religious experience might fit into the levels of his hierarchy. After doing this get them to draw up a short hierarchy of what they

think are religious needs.

Maslow 1908-1970

Maslow was the son of a Jewish immigrant family and lived in a non Jewish community in Brooklyn, New York. He went to study psychology at the University of Wisconsin. Maslow considered that behaviorism and psychoanalytical theory were too rigid in their application of theory and seemed mainly concerned with illness. He wanted to prove that human beings were capable of something grander than war and prejudice.

Maslow concerned himself with two levels of human functioning. He talked about, "survival tendencies" and "actualization tendencies". The survival tendency is that which drives us towards satisfaction and the need to ensure that we physically and psychologically survive.

The Actualization tendency develops from the survival tendency. This drives the individual to develop special capabilities of a higher order. Maslow called this "growth motivation" as the individual does much more than just "get by". According to Maslow Self Actualization follows a genetic blueprint which includes the ability to appreciate beauty, art and good behaviour as part of the religious belief and behaviour.

In his later life he widened this thinking into attempting to give meaning to life. He thought that these peak experiences were what life was all about. He said that these times had a special flavor that we strove to create again and again. One way to do this is through religious ceremony where, through music, drama and vision, peak experiences can be recreated.

Eysenck 1916-1997

Hans Eysenck was born in Germany in 1916. His parents were actors who divorced when he was only two and Hans was raised by his grandmother. He left Germany when he was 18 when the Nazis came to power because, as an active Jewish sympathizer his life was at risk. He cam to England and studied throughout the war at London University and received his PhD in Psychology in 1940. He became director of the psychology department at The Institute of Psychiatry at the Bethlehem Royal Hospital, London.

Although a prolific writer it has been very difficult to find anything that he has written specifically about religion in relation to his theory. However through his writings we do get little glimpses of his thinking. Raj Persaud broadcaster and consultant psychiatrist at the Maudsley Hospital, writing in the Daily Telegraph on March 24th 2003 talks about some of Eysenck's early work In the article he talks about Eysenck putting much of the cause of mental disorder down to the decline of religious observance. From this and the knowledge that Eysenck was an active Jewish sympathizer, we can conclude that he had some interest in religion.

Chapter 5: Psychological development & the influence of religion on Cognitive development

Cognition is the mental act of processing of knowledge through the senses and learning from it. Cognitive development is the study of how this ability is acquired and developed in the child and what part the environment plays in that process. Much of this area of psychology has been dominated by the Swiss psychologist Jean Piaget (1896 – 1980). Piaget's contribution was to acknowledge that the child was not a passive participant but an active and driving force in the process.

Piaget described children as "enquiring little scientists" who experimented with the environment in which there lived and had the ability to draw conclusions from their experiments. From these experiments children develop schemas or theories about the environment around them. When they came across a new situation or object in their environment they have to assimilate this into their current schema.

Piaget's Stage Theory

Piaget divided cognitive development into four key stages each of which had sub stages. He called these stages in ascending order, sensorimotor stage, the preoperational stage, the concrete operational stage and the formal operational stage. So let's take a closer look at these stages in a little more detail.

The Sensorimotor Stage (0 – 2 years)

This starts at day one of life when the child learns that they have the ability to make sound and that when a sound is made something happens. In the early stages of cognitive development it is believed that the child perceives the world as a series of fleeting images. Once a scene is out of sight it, to the child does not exist. The child has to learn that even out of sight objects continue to exist. Piaget called this the concept of "Object Permanence'.

The Preoperational Stage (2 – 7 years)

At the interface between the sensorimotor and preoperational stages the child has been developing the cognitive skills to understand the environment and their role in it. At this time the child will also be using symbols in the form of words and pictures to represent the world around them. As the names suggests the child has not fully learnt the rules or operations that operate in the world in which the child lives.

Concrete Operational Stage (7 – 12 years)

This stage is mainly characterized by the child achievement of the concepts of conservation and the ability to classify objects according to set criteria. One often sees children at this early ages in this stage sorting toys according to color, size etc. Children also have the ability to think in abstracts.

The Formal Operational stage (12 years and above)

This stage is from 12 years onwards and is aptly named "formal" as the maturing child embarks with the cognitive processes developed into the adult world. The key points at this stage is that the child is able to use abstract representations and problem solve.

What the Critics Say about Piaget's Work

Whilst at the time Paiget's stage theory of cognitive development was seen as a major breakthrough in more recent times the tests and assumptions madc by him have been challenged. In the main these challenges appear to demonstrate that Piaget underestimated the ability of children. Many of the tasks that he tested require more sophisticated skills than originally thought.

Alternatives to Piaget's Theory

The opposition to Piaget has taken several routes but all state that his tests failed in so much as they were not testing one factor of cognition but many. Thus the various routes taken have tried to separate out these tasks and develop tests for them.

Knowledge Acquisition Approaches

The developmental psychologists who hold this view believe that children and adults essentially have the same cognitive abilities but what separates them is the level and extent of that knowledge. Chi (1978) demonstrated with chess players from college and 10 year olds that the ability to remember moves and patterns of play was similar between the two groups whilst the ability to remember random number groups was more pronounced in the 18 year old group. He came to the conclusion that the difference between these two groups was not stages of cognitive development but domain specific knowledge.

The Information Processing Approach

These challengers to Piaget argue that cognitive skills rely on the development of Information Processing Skills. By this they mean the specific ability to gather and analyze information from the environment.

Sociocultural Approaches

Much of what the child learns and the way in which it is learnt is influence by the social setting and culture of the child. Theorists describe children as newcomer to a culture who seeks to become a native by learning how to look at social reality through the lens of culture. This then widens the possibilities of what influences our thought processes amongst which must be the influence of religion

Theories of the Mind

Psychologists have been intrigued as to how the mind develops and a whole raft of experiments have been undertaken to test many hypotheses. These experiments have aimed to study children's knowledge about emotions, beliefs and intentions and have demonstrated that in early childhood the ability to think about what others might think is very limited but once a child starts to interact with others on a large scale, such as going to school or nursery the ability rapidly develops

Bartsch (1995) believes that, as in Piaget's cognitive

development there are stages to the development of metacognition. The first stage is when the child realizes that it has desires and emotions and that these need fulfilling. The second stage is about the age of 3 years when children start to talk about beliefs and thoughts as well as their own desires and they also have the ability to decide if things are true or false. Finally at the age of 4 years children begin to understand how others might see them and their behaviour and that people can believe things that do not exist in reality.

Development of Moral Judgment

Piaget believed that moral development went parallel with their cognitive development. One of the ways that he studied this was by observing children at play. In the first stage he noted that when children participated in "Parallel Play". At this stage each child follows their own private set of rules for play and whilst in the same room with other children do not co operate or participated in other children's play. There is no co operation or competition

By the second stage at the age of about 5 years rules become important to a child's play. These rules tend to be absolute and unchangeable and give to the child a set of certainties by which to judge the action of others. At this stage the child sees actions and results as the deciding factor and not the intention.

By the third stage from the age of 8 years onwards all the rules and conventions have been learnt and the child has the ability to appreciate the rules and conventions of society and use them in co operating with others.

The Work of Lawrence Kohlberg

Kohlberg developed Piaget's work further and look at moral reasoning amongst adolescents and young adults. Like Piaget he looked for universal stages in the development of moral judgments.

Much of his testing was similar to Piaget whereby he set stories that had both intent and result that created dilemmas for the participants. By analyzing the answers Kohlberg (1967/11976) arrived at six stages of moral development which he grouped into three levels. the **Preconventional, Conventional and Postconventional.**

Kohlberg reported that only about 10% of adults actually reached stage 6 and showed clear principled thinking. Kohlberg also conducted his research across cultures and the sexual divide. However this has not stopped other criticizing his work on the basis of culture and male dominance in its language. Kohlberg's work does, however, act as a useful adjunct to that of Piaget.

Erikson:- Emotional & Motivational Development

Key to Erikson's work was the belief that everything that lived has ground plan and that everything has a time for acquisition and ascendancy. At the beginning we have all the emotions and motivations that are required in their basic form. As we grow and develop elements become operational at different points in our lives and may take centre stage. Erickson concentrated of socio emotional development and as a consequence looked more closely at the personality rather than the mental functioning of children. He saw various stages to the emotional development in which conflicting emotions could be taking centre stage. These were

Infancy (0-1 ½) Basic trust vs. Basic mistrust (hope)
Early Childhood (2 – 6) Autonomy vs. shame and doubt (will)
Initiative vs. guilt (purpose)
Childhood (7 – 12) Industry vs. Inferiority (Competence)
Adolescence (13 – 21) Identity vs. role confusion (fidelity)
Young Adult (21 – 35) Intimacy vs. isolation (love)
Adulthood (35 – 60) General activity vs. stagnation (care)
Maturity (60 +) Integrity vs. despair (Wisdom)

Gender Identity, Personality and religious Development

Part of this role identity has to be the beliefs that the role model has. In the early stages of our emotional development that models are often our parents. However, as we develop and expand our relationships our role models change.

Another key aspect in our emotional development is we identify of our gender and the role that gender allows up to play. Erikson talks about the concept of "genital maturity".

At each stage of our emotional development the influence of religion has some effect. How we are cared for, what values shape our parents behaviour all have an impact on how we see ourselves, our sexuality and our sexual behaviour. Most faiths have some taboo over same sex relationships and the perversion of the sexual act. Thus if we are exposed to the such teachings they will have an effect on how we see our sexuality and our sexual behaviour.

The Work of Fowler and the Development of Faith

James Fowler took the work of Piaget, Kohlberg and Erikson and from them and his experience as a Christian minister developed a stage theory of the development of faith.

Pre Stage **Undifferentiated Faith** (birth to 1 ½ years)

For the first year or so of life there is only one God figure in the life of a child and that is the prime carer. All the needs and wants of the child are met by this one figure.

Stage 1 **Introjective – Projective Faith** (2 – 6 years)

The child's awareness is quite centered on themselves. Children at this stage love fairy tales and equate Bible stories on a similar level. Whilst, particularly with boys, the stories are rather gruesome, and contain death and scary incidents they see themselves as immortal and will live for ever, despite the fact that they might have encountered death through relatives and family pets.

Stage 2 **Mythic – Literal Faith** (7 – 12 years)

When talking to children about their view of God a marked similarity to the role of the head of a family. All the stories that the child has heard about in relation to faith are taken at a literal level and their interpretation and imagery is related to the family and culture that the child has been brought up in

Stage 3 **Synthetic – Conventional Faith** (13 – 21 years)

There is a great questioning of faith and belief. This may also be a time of experimentation of other beliefs and denominations. From this will come positive and negative effects, their faith may be enhanced or changed to disbelief.

Stage 4 **Individuative – Reflective Faith** (21 – 35 years)

It is found that adults at this time look for similar groups that have the same values as themselves and want a sup portative environment in which to express their faith and to bring their family up in. There is a deepening of faith at this point and a greater quest to understand the meaning of faith to them and their life.

Stage 5 **Conjunctive Faith** (35 – 60 years)

Not all adults reach these last two stages fully. By this time the adult has achieved and faced challenges and overcome hardships and have been subject to the will of other adults. They will have developed a high moral sense which will have been shaped by their faith and belief

Stage 6 **Universalizing Faith** (60+)

This is a time of anticipation and reflection on life; anticipation on what is to come after death and reflection on a life lived. It may be a time for making amends and pardoning wrongs as well as a time of living a faith in its fullest meaning.

Chapter 6: Social Development & the Influence of Religion on Early Social Development

The social environments in which we develop and operate have a huge impact on us and how we behave. Every time we go to church or attend an activity we not only commune with the people we meet, but we also further refine and update of behaviour within that group.

Attachment Theory

The term attachment is used to describe the behaviour demonstrated between carer and baby so as to seek closeness and security with its carers. Usually this is with the mother as the prime carer and develops mainly out of the provision of food, warmth and a feeling of security, or so we thought! Experiments have demonstrated that attachment does not come from the provision of food alone.

Much of the work in this area was done in the 1950's by John Bowlby. He became interested in attachment when watching babies and children in hospital wards and nurseries, particularly when they were separated from their mothers Bowlby's work was further developed by one of his assistants, Mary Ainsworth (1978), who studied mother and child attachment in Uganda and the USA.

From this she was able develop categories of attachment. The categories were as follows:-

Securely Attached:- When the child shows distress at the mother leaving and seeking interaction when she returns. This may be physical or social.

Insecurely Attached, Avoidant:- These children avoid

interacting with the mother

during reunion. Some ignore the mother altogether, others display mixed interactions.

Insecurely Attached, Ambivalent:- These children show resistance to the mother

during reunion episodes. They seem to flip between the need for physical and non physical interaction.

About 65% of children fall into the first category, 20% into the second and 15% into the third. A more recent study has added a fourth category, **Disorganized.** Here children show contradictory behaviors i.e. **Parenting Styles.**

Parenting is an interactive process between the infant the prime care giver and thus, it is also essential to look at how the prime care giver reacts to the child. Prime care givers of the first category appeared to respond promptly when the baby cried, behaved affectionately when they picked up the baby.

In contrast mothers of the insecurely attached children responded according to their own moods rather than according to the needs of the child. Cuddles were given when they felt like it, rather than when the child fretted.

Frodi (1985) looked at how the child reacted when the mother left. The research found that the child's temperament had influence on the former but not the later. Babies with easy temperaments typically were not distressed when the mother left and greeted her happily when she returned.

Studies suggest that children who are securely attached by the time they enter their second year are better equipped to cope with new experiences. However, it is not certain that the quality of early attachment is directly responsible for their later competence in social settings. This seems to depend more on the relationship the child has with its parents at the time. It may also have something to do with the social pressure the child comes under from their piers.

In summary then, children are not significantly affected by non maternal care. Any negative effects tend to be more emotional, and positive effects are more likely to be social. Cognitive development seems to be at worse unaffected or at best improved. What is not so clear is what happens to children exposed to poorer care provision.

Parenting & Belief

Everyone has been influenced by a belief system and just as this affects our day to day lives so too does it influence how we bring up children. The Judeo/Christian ethic of child rearing is for the child to be brought in a stable relationship where the children are taught to live by the rules of love and respect.

In America, where extremes of faith are found, so too one finds extremes of parenting. For example, the Amish live by a very strict code of living the simple life and have no luxuries. They have a very strict dress code and an ethos of hard work. It is into this that the children are taught to honor their parents and do as they are told. They must sit at table and only speak when spoken too. The rearing of the children, whilst primarily the role of the parents, is shared by the whole community.

These Amish communities are similar to that of the Kibbutz in Israel. Here there is less strict adherence to codes of behaviour but still have a religious ethos and a greater sharing of tasks by the community. This includes the rearing of children.

In most Northern European countries the power of religion over the rearing of children has waned greatly. However, whilst the moral arguments that underpin parenting patterns, may be lost, their effects are still observable.

The advice about parenting that has stood the test of time for centuries no longer seems to fit the bill. The effect has been twofold. Firstly, some religions and denominations have fought a rear guide action and pointed out that this social development in family living will end in disaster for the human race. Secondly, because parents living in this style see that religion condemns them, they see if a meaningless archaic institution with nothing to say to them about their way of life.

Social Interactions

The whole aim of parenting is to produce a socially well adjusted individual who will be able to function in society and be a useful member eventually contribute to that society and rear others to replace the dying generations. We are social animals who survive by co operation and co existence. Norman Triplett noticed in 1898 that cyclists who raced with other cyclists did better than those who just raced against the clock. He went on to study a whole variety of other situations and came up with similar findings. Later the Hawthorn Study, which gave rise to the notion of the Hawthorn effect, namely that when a worker has a passive observer watching what they do, they do in such a way as to be perfect in execution.

For co action to take place Triplett discovered that several things need to be in place. Firstly the person must be skilled in the action that they are undertaking, Secondly the person much not feel inhibited or scared by the presence of others and thirdly, they need to have pride or a spirit of competition in what they are undertaking.

A contemporary of Triplett, Gustave Lebon, was also looking at coaction but from the point of view of how people behave when in a crowd. His seminal book called, "The Crowd" (1895) Lebon asserts that the crowd is always inferior to the individual when it comes to behaviour. He asserted that when a crowd, especially when roused, started to act social norms went out the window.

To explain this behaviour psychologists have coined the term "Deindividuation". This is when certain situations can minimize the individual identity of people and thus reduce their sense of public accountability and in so doing allow them to commit aggressive or abnormal acts.

Bystander Effect

In the gospels we read of the story told by Jesus of the "good Samaritan" who was the only person, amongst the many who passed by, who went to the aid of a man who was lying in the roadside after being attacked by robbers. This is the earliest recorded event of a phenomenon called the "Bystander effect".

Atkinson (2003) describes this as:-

The effect that people are less likely to help a person in difficulty When others are present"

Group Dynamics

This is the study of how groups develop and the role that people play within such groups. Groups form for a whole variety of reasons, some are brought together by others whilst others are a coalition of people who have come together to perform given tasks. Within such groups some people will be appointed whilst others may offer to take on roles. The study of a religious congregation offers quite and useful glimpse into the way that groups operate.

Externally Designated groups are formed when others have brought the group into being for some purpose. Often these groups are large such as a race or nation, whilst at other times they can be small and brought together to achieve some task or purpose.

Another type of group is when people feel strongly about a subject or situation and find other people of a similar mind and come together to achieve some aim. These are called "Pressure Groups" and are formed to put pressure on another group to achieve their aim or put their point of view across. Once the aim is achieved or the purpose has passed the group dissolves.

Often within groups, especially when they are large and externally designated, one finds the development of "Sub Groups". These are small groups of people who, whilst sharing the overall aims of the larger group have particular agendas that they wish to pursue. Despite why a group is formed, all groups need a leader. Leaders may be externally designated by the people that formed the group; through election from within the group, or evolve from the group. Whatever the means used to get a leader, there are some qualities that a leaders needs. Chief amongst these has to be that the group believes in the leader and has trust. Often leaders are charismatic and have the ability to make people believe in them and follow their leadership. They must have good people skills and be good communicators. They must also have authority. By this one means that they must have the ability to see things through and take the group with them. If at any time these aspects are lost or perceived to have been diminished, then the group may lose confidence in the leader. In such situations an anti leader will often appear. This person may be covert in their challenge or overt. By far the most dangerous is the covert anti leader.

Others take on other roles such as the group comic, always relieving stress by jokes and fun; the group secretary, taking on the role of organizing and monitoring the groups performance. Then there is the group scapegoat, perhaps not a member of the group but a person who the group can agree on as the person who causes all their troubles or act as a but for their own failings. No one person has a monopoly on a role but may play various roles in various groups. It is an astute person who comes into a group, defines what roles people have developed for themselves and adopts a role that is not filled.

Group Activity

Think of a group that you are in and:

1) Try to define what sort of group it is

2) What type of leader you have

3) What roles people played within the group

Compliance & Obedience

Whilst in groups we may find that we do not always agree with what the group as a whole are doing. Sometimes we go along with the group, even though we do not agree with the line of action. Where an individual is at odds with the group often the group will put pressure on the individual. The need for conformity in a group is essential for the good working of the group. How that pressure affects the individual was studied by Asch (1958). His findings astonished most people at the time because he found that we can be so pressured by group members to go along with group action and behaviour, even when we know it to be wrong.

Asch thought that this was not conformity, for this means submitting to the group will both in body and mind, What he observed was compliance, namely that the individual went along with the group but not actually changing one's mind as to the validity of the individual action.

Group Norms and Beliefs

Key to a group sticking together and working effectively is the idea of having some standard norms and beliefs that bind them together. For example, members of a church have a basis common belief in God and in Jesus Christ. This belief is what caused them to come together. Superimposed on this are beliefs about how worship should take place and these then allow the group to have a set of normative behaviors that constitute how worship should be conducted. The effect of these beliefs and norms are to make the bonds with the group members strong and to make the working of the group easy

"Groupthink" is a type of thinking found amongst very cohesive groups where members want to reach some common view point on specific issues. Often this "groupthink" produces decisions that are not based on logic or logical thought but out of a need to find consensus. This often lead to faulty decision making which in the end had an adverse effect on the group. Janis (1982) found that "groupthink" occurs when the following conditions are present:-

When the group is very cohesive

When the group has little contact with quality sources of information

When the group leader is clearly in favour of a certain course of action

When the decision is made under stress and in a hurry

When there is a common ideology amongst the members

What this tends to show is that dissention in a group is in fact a good thing. However, if left unchecked it could destroy the group.

Summary

WE have seen that the social environment in which we develop and operate have a huge impact on our behaviour in society. Our upbringing and our faith have a major impact on how we behave in society. We saw that this process starts from the very beginning of our life on the day we are born and is a lifelong process. We are the product of our upbringing and social interactions about which faith has a lot to say and to do.

Chapter 7: The brain, prayer, meditation and healing

Introduction

Dr. Herbert Benson(1976) in his book "The relaxation Response" believes that prayer elicits the same biochemical response as does the process of relaxation; affecting the production of epinephrine and other corticotrophins, all of which have the effect of lowering blood pressure, reducing heart rate and respiration. It has also been found that these hormones also affect immune functioning. Other studies have shown that the relaxation response and spirituality are both controlled by the amygdala-a small structure within the brain that-together with the hippocampus and hypothalamus, also located in the brain-make up the limbic system. It is the limbic system that controls emotions, sexual pleasure, intense memory and spirituality.

The Brain and the Power of Prayer

Stories of the power of prayer and healing take three forms. Firstly, prayer and religious involvement can help people cope with sickness. Secondly, prayer can pray an important part in arresting the progress of certain illnesses such as cancer and heart disease. Thirdly, from a combination of medication and prayer some people have been healed.

Research has also shown that spirituality and religion do play an important role in the maintenance of health and healing.

The Word of Newberg

In his book, Why God Won't Go Away, Newberg hypothesis is that biology compels the spiritual urge. Newberg says that on the one hand the concept of God is part of who we are and what we experience in our brains; however, we do have a clear answer as to whether it was put there by God or developed over millions of years of evolution.

Some of the early studies that Newberg undertook looked at the electrical changes in the brain and how prayer and meditation affected body function such as heart rate and blood pressure. For the most part these studies showed a large number of changes take place in the brain when we pray. The studies showed that a number of areas of the brain act together. There are both cognitive and emotional elements involved. in prayer. The frontal lobe, which seems to be responsible for focusing or attention behaviour, becomes increasingly activated. This makes sense because prayer is a focusing activity. Another area of the brain involved in prayer and meditation is the parietal lobe; located toward the back, top part of the brain. This area is sometimes referred to as the orientation part of the brain.

Such studies have given Newberg a model of what occurs in the brain during prayer and meditation. With the advent of brain imaging technologies other studies have been undertaken to see if this model has any value in fact. Such imaging studies have supported Newbergs model and demonstrated that is prayer is an active process that affects the emotional part s of the brain and some of the brainstem functions that regulate heart beat and blood pressure.

Thus, what distinguishes Newberg's research from all others, is that he has not only an eye on the material but also the spiritual experience of prayer and meditation. Religion gives us a different way of looking at the world in which we live.

Meditation and the Brain

Using imaging techniques again Newberg recruited a group of people who were very experienced in meditation and prayer and brought them into his laboratory to observe brain activity as they practiced. Newberg chose a group of Tibetan Buddhist monks and a group of nuns all of whom had about 20 to 25 years of experience of meditation. Although there are a variety of approaches to meditation this did not appear to affect the study.

The results were consistent with the other models that Newberg had developed, I.e. an increase activity in the frontal lobe of the brain associated with attention and a relative decrease activity in the orientation part of the brain. The results appear to show that meditation or prayer has the same effect and uses the same part of the brain.

The Meaning of Newbergs work

The conclusion from Newbergs' work could be that there is nothing more to the spiritual experience than brain function. Others take the opposite few and think that Newberg's work demonstrate that God has "hard wired" the brain so that God can be worshipped. What Newburg points out is that all our experiences have to be perceived in some way through brain activity and function and, thus you cannot rule out the brain from the experience.

There is no doubt that prayer and meditation do produce specific patterns of brain behaviour that are not seen in any other activity. What is happening is that parts of the brain are behaving in ways not seen in normal brain activity.

That the power of prayer and meditation lies in the ability to provide the believers with experimental evidence that seems to "prove" that the guarantees made in myth and scripture are true. Rituals allow participants to taste, if only for a moment, the transcendent spiritual unity that all religions promise". We are able to "taste" this spiritual unity because of the neurological processes and because of memory associations we have in the brain which are triggered by the symbolic language and repetitive actions of our religious rituals. In short, worship involving prayer and meditation evoke feelings and thoughts associate with hope and love. Our brain is wired for rituals and that is why worship is good for us.

Near Death Experience

The term "Near Death Experience" refers to a wide range of experiences reported by some people who have nearly died or who have thought they were going to die. Whilst there are many similarities in what they feel and see there is no one single experience that all have in common. However, many report of seeing bright lights, having traveled down a tunnel to a bright light and having out of body experiences. What is common to all is that such events are life changing for those who experience them. Such experiences do not happen to everyone who nearly dies or who has been resuscitated. Research seems to indicate that between 18% and 25% of those questioned after such an event have had a near death experience. In the main, the younger the subject is the more likely they are to have an experience.

The term Near Death Experience was popularized in the 1970's by Elizabeth Kubler-Ross and Raymond Moody. Kubler-Ross (1977) had become well known for her work on death and dying and described experiences that some people had that reassured them that there was something after life. However, it was the work of Raymond Moody in his book, Life after Life that really developed the study into such experiences. Moody interviewed several thousand people who had been resuscitated and questioned them on what they had experienced. Of those who had had such experiences he was able to produce a list of common experiences. These were:-

Noises similar to bells or buzzers
A sense of total peace or blissfulness
A feeling of floating out of the body and observing it from above
Moving through a tunnel towards a bright light
Meeting dead relatives
Seeing a spiritual figure (Christ, angels, Buddha or similar)
Seeing one's life pass before one's eyes

Pim Van Lommel has been conducting a longitudinal study into 344 resuscitated patients to see how their Near Death Experiences would shape their lives. At the outset Van Lommel thought that if the experiences were purely physiological there would be a common experience to all who reported NDE's This proved not to be the case and led him to believe that psychological factors must interplay with the physiological. As stated earlier, Van Lommel found that NDE experiences are not confined to resuscitated patients. Similar experiences could be induced through electrical stimulation of the temporal lobe during neurosurgery for epilepsy. It could also be induced with high carbon dioxide levels in the blood such as when a person hyperventilates.

Whilst Moody is convinced that Near Death Experiences are evidence of the conscious existing separately from the brain, and thus life after death, Skeptics, believe that all of these changes can be explained by changes in the neurochemistry of the brain as the brain gradually degrades in death.

The Enduring Effects of Near Death Experiences

Atwater (2004) found that only 20% of those who she interviews and reported NDE had no life changing effects. The majority, 80% claimed radical changes, almost as if they had become another person. Many saw the survival of death as a privilege and to glimpse what they thought of as heaven as a piece of "Amazing Grace".

Psychological Effects

Atwater has observed that it takes about seven years for most people who have an NDE to integrate it into their common experience of life, i.e. to be able to understand it and talk about the effects that it has one their lives. Seven major elements seem to be common to all who reported changes. These areas follow:-

Unconditional love. Where they feel loving towards all who they meet and find it difficult to hate

A lack of Boundaries. New frames or reference become common that govern the individual behaviour. There is a greater tolerance and more understanding about others beliefs and values

Timelessness. There becomes an increasing emphasis of living for the moment and the rejection of schedules and time to govern how one lives

More Psychic. The individual experiences more extrasensory perception and various types of psychic phenomena not common in ordinary life; having visions and dreaming prophetic dreams

Reality Switching. Hard driving individuals become easy going. Those that are materialistic dwell more on aesthetic values

The Soul as Self. Most commonly the individual talks about a more spiritual way of looking at life and how they live it.

Modes of Communication. What was one foreign becomes familiar, what was once familiar becomes foreign. Rationale of any kind tends to lose its logic and NDE's begin to think more abstractly and in grandiose terms. New ways of using language even new vocabularies develop

Physiological Changes after Near Death Experiences

J Raichle (2004) has shown that such imaging has allowed us to see that original thinking uses different areas of the brain from mundane thinking. In those who have had NDE's there appears to be a paradigm shift in the areas of the brain that are used for normal thinking. Different areas of the brain appear to be dominant in those who have had NDE's and those who have not. Raichle reports observable changes in the brain structurally making the brain being more able to data cluster and towards a more creative way of thinking. This shift in brain activity seems to cause the person to experience visions, hearing voices and other such phenomena associated with spiritual experiences. Reviewing this evidenced one comes back again to the work of Newberg and the question as to whether the brain is "hard wired" to experience God or not. What is sure is that we are getting closer to understanding how we experience God and religion.

Cellular Memory in Organ Transplant Patients

Leslie Takeucji (2004) has written a literature search of this subject. In her work as a physio (physical) therapist she has been acutely aware of the relationship between the brain, body and emotions in the way that people cope with pain and the whole process of healing. She was anxious to see what part memory played in the process. i.e. memory of pain and the effect it has on the process of healing. Current theory of memory is that it is a brain function and that memory cells, although not specific to a region of the brain, reside close to areas where function exists.

Takeuchi started to notice an increasing number of articles, mainly anecdotal, that were describing events that seemed to point to another form of memory, cellular memory. What was most striking to her was to see the number of organ transplant patients who later experienced changes in personality traits, tastes for food, music, activities and even sexual preference. It may well be, according to Takeuchi, that memory is too complex a subject to be just a brain activity and it may be part of a world of quantum sub particle systems that affects not only the brain but the body .

Candace Pert,(2004) believes, " memories are not only stored in the brain but in the psychosomatic network extending into the body .. All the way out along pathways to internal organs and the very surface of our own skin". After having discovered neuropeptides in all body tissues, Pert suggests that through cellular receptors, thoughts or memories may remain unconscious or become conscious, raising the possibility of physiological connections between memories, organs and the brain.

Paul Pearsall (1996), a psychoneuro immunologist and author of the Heart Code has looked at the transference of memory through organ transplantation. After interviewing nearly 150 heart and other organ transplant recipients, Pearsall proposes the idea that cells of living tissue have the capacity to remember. Together with Schwarz and Russek, Pearsall conducted a study published in the spring of 2002 in the Journal of Near Death Experiences entitled, "Changes in Heart Transplant Recipients That Parallel the Personalities of Their Donor". The following are just a few samples from the many cases cited.

In one case, an 18 year old boy who wrote poetry, played music and composed songs, was killed in an automobile accident. A year later his parents came across an audiotape of a song he had written entitled, "Danny, My Heart is Yours", which was about how he "was destined to die and give his heart to someone". The donor recipient, "Danny", of his heart was an 18 year old girl called Daniella. When she met the donor's parents, they played some of his music and she, despite never having heard the song, was able to complete the phrases.

A 29 year old Lesbian and a fast food junkie received a heart from 19 year old woman vegetarian who was "man mad". The recipient reported after her operation that meat made her sick and she was no longer attracted to women, In fact, she became engaged to marry a man. Another amazing story, reported by Pearsall, is that of an eight year old girl who received the heart of a ten year old girl who had died from injuries received in a brutal attack. After the transplant the recipient had horrible nightmares of a man murdering the donor. The dreams were so traumatic that psychiatric help was sought. The girls images were so specific that the psychiatrist and the mother notified the police. According to the psychiatrist, using the descriptions from the little girl, they found the murderer. He was easily convicted with the evidence the patient provided. She was able to describe the time, weapon, place of the attack, the cloths he wore and what the little girl he killed had said to him. All proved to be completely accurate.

The Church and New Perspectives on Healing

What has also become clear is that science, seen in the 1950's as holding the possibility of being able to cure all has singularly failed to do so. This has led to the remarkable resurgence in the practice Christian healing.

It is important to make a delineation between Christian healing and Spiritual healing. According to the Arch Bishops Commission on Healing in 1958, healing is:-

The Pastoral and sacramental ministry of healing brings an assurance to the

Patient that God is acting both within their inner most being and through those

Who are treating them. It helps to break down barriers deep inside the
Personality which stand in the way of healing.

Spiritual healing is not a Christian belief but relies on the spirit world removing evil influences from the individual and changing the aura that surrounds an individual. In so doing the person becomes who and well again.

Christian healing is more than treating symptoms. It is a process that restores harmony and balance within and between people. Christians believe that Jesus is the source and agent for this healing. Through his suffering and divine power to heal he wishes all to be free from the agents of sickness.

The use of prayer and meditation are seen as being active agents for change that can affect health. Many of the compounds of oils used by the church in anointing have been found to have medicinal properties one wonders how long it will be before we find that confession and the laying on of hands will also have some effect. Where the church has made healing an almost total preserve has been in the field of Hospice care. Much of the work in this field has been pioneered in the last two centuries by committed Christian people. Hospices offer specific care for the dying in the context of Christian love.

Chapter 8: Stress, life events and religion

Introduction

Stress may be defined as the experiencing of events that are perceived as endangering one physical and psychological well being. Stress has two elements to it. Firstly, there is the actual event, referred to as the ***Stressor,*** and then the way the individual responds to the stressor referred to as ***The Stress Response.*** This response may be physical and or psychological. The stressors can classified as being either controlled, I.e. those we expect and can do something about, uncontrolled such as traumatic events or those that are self induced through internal conflict.

Stress and Change

Many of the situations or events that cause stress are due to change. In fact stress is synonymous with change. It does not matter is the change is good or bad either will cause stress. The changes can be perceived or actual physical or mental, all cause STRESS

Two early researches who looked into how changes affects stress where Holmes and Rahe (1967). In an attempt to measure these events they looked at thousands of lives and tried to catalogue what was happening in their lives prior to them suffering such things as heart attacks or strokes. As marriage appeared to be a critical event of change for most people they placed this event in the middle of the scale and gave it a value of 50. They then asked 400 people of various sages and backgrounds to compare other events that caused change and place them in relation to marriage. They were then asked to assign a value to each event.

This stress inventory had a major effect on the management of stress and research into it. It demonstrated that the most serious events that caused stress were, as thought, mainly negative, but also demonstrated that positive events did have some harmful effect

Group activity:

STRESS SCALE FOR ADULTS

In the following table you can look up representative changes

in your life and see how much stress value each of these changes is adding to your life.

NOTE ANY ITEM THAT YOU MAY HAVE EXPERIENCED IN THE LAST TWELVE MONTHS.

Then, total up your score.

(Adapted from the "Social Readjustment Rating Scale" by Thomas Holmes and Richard Rahe. This scale was first published in the "Journal of Psychosomatic Research", Copyright 1967, vol.II p. 214. It is used by permission of Pergamon Press Ltd.)

Stress Scale for Adults

DEATH OF SPOUSE	100
DIVORCE	100
MENOPAUSE	100
SEPARATION FROM LIVING PARTNER	60
JAIL TERM OR PROBATION	60
DEATH OF CLOSE FAMILY MEMBER OTHER THAN SPOUSE	60
SERIOUS PERSONAL INJURY OR ILLNESS	60
MARRIAGE OR ESTABLISHING LIFE PARTNERSHIP	45
FIRED AT WORK	45
MARITAL OR RELATIONSHIP RECONCILIATION	45
RETIREMENT	40
CHANGE IN HEALTH OF IMMEDIATE FAMILY MEMBER	40
WORK MORE THAN 40 HOURS PER WEEK	40
PREGNANCY OR CAUSING PREGNANCY	35

SEX DIFFICULTIES	35
GAIN OF NEW FAMILY MEMBER	35
BUSINESS OR WORK ROLE CHANGE	35
CHANGE IN FINANCIAL STATE	35
DEATH OF A CLOSE FRIEND (not a family member)	35
CHANGE IN NUMBER OF ARGUMENTS WITH SPOUSE OR LIFE PARTNER	30
MORTGAGE OR LOAN FOR A MAJOR PURCHASE	30
FORECLOSURE OF MORTGAGE OR LOAN	25
SLEEP LESS THAN 8 HOURS PER NIGHT	25
CHANGE IN RESPONSIBILITIES AT WORK	25
TROUBLE WITH IN-LAWS, OR WITHCHILDREN	25
OUTSTANDING PERSONAL ACHIEVEMENT	25
SPOUSE BEGINS OR STOPS WORK	20
BEGIN OR END SCHOOL	
PREGNANCY OR CAUSING PREGNANCY	35
SEX DIFFICULTIES	35
GAIN OF NEW FAMILY MEMBER	35

BUSINESS OR WORK ROLE CHANGE	35
CHANGE IN FINANCIAL STATE	35
DEATH OF A CLOSE FRIEND (not a family member)	35
CHANGE IN NUMBER OF ARGUMENTS WITH SPOUSE OR LIFE PARTNER	30
MORTGAGE OR LOAN FOR A MAJOR PURCHASE	30
FORECLOSURE OF MORTGAGE OR LOAN	25
SLEEP LESS THAN 8 HOURS PER NIGHT	25
CHANGE IN RESPONSIBILITIES AT WORK	25
TROUBLE WITH IN-LAWS, OR WITHCHILDREN	25
OUTSTANDING PERSONAL ACHIEVEMENT	25
SPOUSE BEGINS OR STOPS WORK	20
BEGIN OR END SCHOOL	20

TOTAL SCORE ______________________________

We have asked you to look at the last twelve months of changes in your life. This may surprise you. It is crucial to understand, however, that a major change in your life has effects that carry over for long periods of time. It is like dropping a rock into a pond. After the initial splash, you will experience ripples of stress. And these ripples may continue in your life for at least a year.

So, if you have experienced total stress within the last twelve months of 250 or greater, even with normal stress tolerance, you may be OVERSTRESSED. Persons with Low Stress Tolerance may be OVERSTRESSED at levels as low as 150.

OVERSTRESS will make you sick. Carrying too heavy a stress load is like running your car engine past the red line; or leaving your toaster stuck in the "on" position; or running a nuclear reactor past maximum permissible power. Sooner or later, something will break, burn up, or melt down. What breaks depends on where the weak links are in your physical body. And this is largely an inherited characteristic.

Characteristics of Stressful Events

Looking at the stress inventory it is possible to see the three groups identified earlier, I.e. those vents that were controlled, uncontrolled or caused by internal conflict. The most common causes of stress are those that one feels we have n0 control over. In the main these tend to be traumatic events such as an accidents natural disasters or trauma to one self esteem. 2004 saw the worst natural disaster of modern times when a tsunami hit the shores of countries coasting on the Indian Ocean. In the press reports that followed this dreadful events reporters talked about the survivors wandering the streets in dazed states, totally disorientated and unable to comprehend what had happened.

These reports mirrored the finds of Horowitze (1986) who looked at how people had responded to such events as earthquakes and the like. Often these people appear to be on the verge of collapse both physically and mentally. They are unable to initiate or comply with simple tasks but do follow impassively simple orders or instructions. Similar behaviour has also been noted in rape victims who are often described as being like "rag dolls" sitting impassively, not thinking or responding to the world around them and even forgetting to do such things as eat and drink. In the main their attention is focused on the event and they often repeat the story of the event to who ever will listen and sometimes event to themselves.

Koss and Oesten (1998) Studied how people responded to physical and sexual abuse. Their study showed that such attacks often lead to the individuals suffering from depression and a loss of self esteem. In others there was a complete psychological change in the individual, being withdrawn, unable to manage their lives and often not liking to mix with society. Burnham (1988) found that, in severe cases, acute mental illness developed and the victim took on a personal where what ever happened adversely to the individual was always the fault of the event. This so called "Victim Culture" gave cause to what ever happened there after.

Fortunately, the majority do not suffer such severe events, however, the events that we do suffer demonstrate four characteristics, controllability, predictability, change and conflict.. In each case we conduct an appraisal as to how much we perceive these events to threaten us. Thus, it is important to look at these in a little more detail

Controllability

Controllability of an event is the degree to which we think we can stop the thing happening or affecting us. The more uncontrollable we feel the even to be the more it will cause us stress

Predictability

Predictability also allows us to reduce the degree of stress that we suffer. Predictability allows the individual to prepare for the event.

Major Life Changing Events

In the Holmes & Rahe list all events, be they good or bad, require the individual to undergo a number of changes in their life. As stated earlier negative events have a much greater impact than positive, but all change is stressful. There are some common physical responses to stress, These include:

Brain overstress, the individual suffers from fatigue, aches and pains, crying spells, depression, anxiety attacks and sleep disturbance

Gastrointestinal disorders, these may be ulcers, stomach cramps and diahorrea, colitis and irritable bowel syndrome

Cardiovascular disorders, high blood pressure, heart attacks, abnormal heart beat and cerebral vascular accidents (strokes)

Skin, rashes and itchy skin, changes in skin quality

Immune system, an increase in infections and neoplasm (growths internal or external)

Internal Conflict

Internal conflict refers to those events that we think about either consciously or unconsciously that have remained unresolved. These too are often events that relate to change and choices that one has to make in life. These could be such things as choosing between options for jobs, which person to support in an argument or whether to give some information that could cause trouble for you or an individual in the future.

Atkinson (2003) talks about conflict occurring internally under four key areas. These are:

Independence versus dependence. In difficult situations we often would like someone to made the decisions for us, but are also we are told to stand on our own two feet. We also value the chance to do something independently but know that in so doing we may offend those around us

Intimacy versus isolation. The desire to be close to someone and share physical and mental intimacy but being afraid that what is shared may cause the individual to use it against one and cause hurt and upset

Cooperation versus competition. We live in a competitive world and life advances depend on competition but for things to succeed we need to work cooperatively. This results in rivalry and one is not sure if others are working for your good or your downfall

Expression of impulses versus moral standards. Every human being has impulses to behave in a way that could be considered antisocial. What stops such behaviour is the fact that one might be caught or the fact that the behaviour will conflict with moral standards set by ourselves or society.

These four areas present the greatest potential for serious conflict. Trying to find a workable compromise between opposing motives can cause considerable stress.

The Physiology of Stress

The brain produces two groups of chemical messengers, those that make us fell happy and energetic and those that make us feel sad and listless. In normal living, these tend to be kept in balance and, as a consequence, we feel pretty good about life. However, when stressed, there is an increase in the production of sad messengers which distress the brain.

If the production of such chemicals is prolonged this has a detrimental effect on brain function. The individual often complains of feeling listless, unable to cope, an increase in aches and pains and a general feeling of life overwhelming them. This often leads on to anxiety, depression and a general reduction in the ability to cope with life. It appears that our ability to cope with the stresses of daily living depends on our genetic inheritance to produce enough of the happy messengers to balance the production of sad messengers. This ability to cope is referred to as the Stress tolerance

We see these genetic differences in the way that people are affected by predictable stressful events.

Chemical Messengers and their function

Three chemicals make up the happy messengers in the brain. These are Serotonin, Noradrenalin and Dopamine.

Serotonin has the function of regulating sleep. When Serotonin is high then we sleep, when Melatonin is high we are awake. The Serotonin / Melatonin interchange also affect temperature of the body, ensuring that at night the body is cooler than during the day by up to 1C. This rise and fall in body temperature induces sleep.

Whilst many people havc heard of adrenalin, nor adrenalin is not so well know. This chemical has a large number of functions in the brain and nervous system. However, in relation to stress, Noradrenalin sets the energy levels of the body. Proper functioning of Noradrenalin in the brain is essential for the person to feel energized.

Dopamine is the natural pain relief stimulator in the brain. Like morphine and heroin not only does it relieve pain it also produced a feeling of general well being. Recent research has shown that Production of Dopamine occurs near to the points in the brain where Endorphins are produced. Endorphins are the natural pain suppressers and are responsible for our moment to moment awareness of pain. When Dopamine production is suppressed then the production of Endorphins also reduces and the person starts to a greater degree of aches and pains.

Dopamine also appears to stimulate the pleasure centre in the brain. This area of the brain allows one to enjoy life and feel good. When stress interferes with the Dopamine function the Pleasure Centre becomes inoperative.

Psychological Reactions to Stress

These changes in brain chemistry produce behavioural changes in the individual. These include, anxiety, depression, aggression and cognitive impairment. Depending on the degree of stress will affect which of these changes in behaviour will be demonstrated. The most common early behavioural change associated with Stress is anxiety. In its simplest form Anxiety is characterized by an increase in the amount of Adrenalin circulating in the body. This increase causes the person to be "on edge" twitchy and unable to sleep and concentrate. In prolonged cases of exposure to stress a set of anxiety related symptoms occur which are often referred to as Post Traumatic Stress Disorder.

These prolong effects include the following:-
A feeling of detachment from daily life
A lack of emotional reaction to events
Listlessness
Flashback of the stressful event
Sleep disturbances
Difficulty in concentration
A certain amount of "jumpiness"

Another common reaction to stress is anger and aggression. Direct aggression toward the cause of the frustration may nor be possible or wise. The person may not know what to attack but feel they must attack something. When a direct attack is not possible the aggression may be displaced, i.e., turned towards something else..

A juxtaposition to Aggression and anger is the apathy and depression. If the stressor continues for a prolonged period this is more likely to be the response that the person suffers.

In learned helplessness the person appears to be apathetic, withdrawn and totally unable to respond to uncontrolled events. The person appears to have given up in the face of the events.

Cognitive impairment often is associated with high levels of emotional arousal such as anger and aggression as well as from the thoughts that the stressor induces. The effect of cognitive impairment over a prolonged period is to induce very rigid behaviour patterns in the individual having the effect of increasing the stress when these behaviour are challenged.

Coping with Stress

In looking at how people cope with stress, psychologists have identified two major ways that people use to reduce the effects of stress. These are Problem Focused and Emotional Focused coping.

Problem-Focused Coping is where the person defines what the problems are and then attempts to generate alternative strategies that will reduce the stress. In so doing they weigh up the benefits and costs of each alternative. Eventually the person decides which solution best resolves the stress for them individually.

Emotional Focused Coping attempts to stop negative emotions overwhelming the individual and thus, causing them to be unable to solve their own problems. Emotional focusing may be achieved wither by looking at changing behaviors or analyzing cognitively what is happening (Moos 1988)

Emotional Focused Coping, whilst effective, does not appear to be as successful as that of Behavioural Focused Coping. Longitudinal studies have shown that those using this approach appear to have longer and deeper depressions.

Stress and Religious Belief

Research by Moen and others over the last decade has shown that having a religious belief and using prayer and meditation do have a positive effect on the reduction of stress. In particular meditation and prayer fit in quite well with the focusing strategies described above.

Prayer works in two ways. Firstly personal prayer, asking the deity to help with or remove the stressor allowed the individual to share the problem that is causing the stress, albeit with an unseen individual.

The second way that prayer can be used is through requests for prayers at public worship. Increasingly in public worship people are asked for prayers. These tend to be times of sharing good and bad news within the religious family. By using this vehicle the person suffering from stress is able to share with their fellow worshippers the stressor that they have in an appropriate and socially acceptable way. The individual will derive from this much peer support.

Meditation, on the other hand, tends to fit in well with the Behavioural Focusing. By being able to take time out and concentrate on a specific issue the person is able to be very focused on this issues that lay before them. They are able to block out extraneous thoughts and feeling and focus on the essentials of the stressor. As a consequence they are able to see the wood for the trees and produce a strategy for change that will fit the situation that they face.

Loss and Grieving

In the process of grieving, each individual spends a different length of time working through each stage and will express each stage will a different degree of intensity.

Elizabeth Kubler- Ross (1976) identifies five key stages that grieving people tend to pass through. Whilst these five stages are always present they are not necessarily passed through in the same order.

The Five Stages of Grieving

1) Denial

The first reaction on learning that someone is dead, terminally ill is to deny the reality of the situation. There tends to be an overwhelming of the emotions and the person has bouts controllable crying and may even go into shock.

2) Anger

As the emotional shock of the news wears off the person starts to feel angry and the reality of the situation starts to dawn on the individual. The anger tends to be unfocused and aimed at anything or body that happens to be near at the time.

3) Bargaining

The usual reaction to feeling this loss of control in ones life is to try and regain it in some way. In those that terminally ill one finds the individual trying to seek second opinions, looking for alternative therapies and possibly bargaining with God that if they become more religious could the burden be taken away from them.

4) Depression

This occurs to the change in circumstance. The grieving person feels intensely sad and find that the decision that have to be made almost impossible to do. Funeral arrangements, costings, who needs to be informed and the like all become difficult to the think about and do. Even the help from friends and relatives is impossible to cope with at times.

5) Acceptance

Getting to this stage can take a few weeks or even a few years and in some cases is never reached. Acceptance comes when the changes that the death have caused become part of a new lifestyle. The person becomes calm and more organized and looks back on what has happened with a fondness for the person and a sense of closure on the life of the individual.

At times when deaths are not expected or caused through unexpected circumstances the individuals want to make something good come out of what they see as evil. In the case of where a baby dies in utero the offering of the fetus for stem cell research may offer the parents a means of making sense of the tragedy they have gone through. When a child is murdered parents may set up a trust or help line for parents in similar situations. In all cases these acts help the grieving individuals to come to terms with their loss

A more recent review by Debra Moore (2004) has reduced these stages to four and has also found that, over the years, society has put a greater pressure on people to get back to normal patterns of living. There is also a greater use of counseling and support to help people go through the grieving process

Printed in the United States
49642LVS00002B/556-585

9 781424 101481